HEAR MORE FROM
FEATURED CONTRIBUTORS

"I retired in 2012 and felt that it was time for me to give back what gifts that were given to me. I am having a blast!! This is not about me but about them. My hope is that before I leave this life, I am able to give more than I have taken."

**–Michael Kogutek, former Chairman,
Executive Coaches of Orange County**

"First, I was curious. Then I was inspired."

**–Michael Vaughn, attorney and
Former City Councilman**

"The world is full of people who want to be a force for good. They sometimes just don't know where to start."

–Shawn Wehan, founder of Givsum, Inc.

"From each of the organizations I've supported, I've learned more than I imagined and gained more than I've given."

–Victoria Collins, retired Businesswoman

"I had no idea, literally no idea, about the impact that my decision to create and start Bracken's Kitchen would have on so many people."

–Bill Bracken, founder of Bracken's Kitchen

"My fellow entrepreneurs, it's not about doing more. It's about being more of yourself."

**–Stephanie Courtillier,
founder of Integrous Women**

Living a Richer Life

REAL STORIES OF LASTING IMPACT

Richard J. Ward, CFP®

Published by
Richard J. Ward, CFP® Irvine, California

Production Team
Patricia Beaulieu, editorial project manager, njr productions
Nancy Ratkiewich, book design/production, njr productions
Bridget Soden Mills, cover design, Creative Vortex, Inc.

For general information on other products and services, please visit the website: https://www.richardwardwealthadvisory.com.

ISBN: 9798218072865 Paperback
ISBN: 9798218120719 eBook

Printed in the United States of America
10 9 8 7 6 5 4 3 2 1

DEDICATION

This book is dedicated to the countless volunteers, philanthropists, and other leaders (and certainly all who have shared their stories here) who have found their way to helping others learn, grow, and thrive, and in doing so, are in their own ways living a much richer life.

CONTENTS

CHAPTER THREE
NON-PROFIT FOUNDERS/LEADERS   **69**

FOREWORD

Throughout my 20+ years of management in the financial services industry, and having coached well over 200 financial advisors/planners, the retirement conversation focused on not outliving savings and planning for events that come with growing older. A good financial planner will help you develop a roadmap for successfully managing your wealth in retirement.

When I met Richard, the conversation shifted from the expected retirement planning conversation to the unexpected one. Until then, I hadn't had the pleasure of meeting an advisor who talked about helping their clients find significance or purpose in their lives, especially in their retirement years. Coming from a financial advisor, this conversation seemed somewhat foreign. Yes, they can advise whether one can afford to purchase that vacation home in a far-off land, but nothing about the psychology of how one might "feel" when they finally decide to say goodbye to the career that had provided so much self-worth and fulfillment.

The concept of living a richer life through service and philanthropy sounded fantastic and possibly somewhat esoteric to most, including myself. How does one discover their passion, the right organization to help, the right fit for their skills, and an introduction to help them get started?

Working with Richard over the past 11 years, I realized that perhaps I needed answers to these same questions. How will I feel when it's time to retire; how do I feel now that I am an empty nester and life is somewhat quieter; where will I find my purpose and fulfillment?

I've had the pleasure of witnessing Richard help his clients, friends, and colleagues discover their version of a richer life. I've experienced first-hand, although he may not realize it, his gentle guidance to my own discovery and path. His passion is infectious, and his search for knowledge has resulted in the stories shared in this book. The individuals in these stories are like people you may know; the neighbor next door, a current or former colleague, or an acquaintance you met through friends. They are the ones who are making a difference in our communities. They have discovered their purpose and passion, resulting in a richer life for themselves and, perhaps more importantly, for others. In reading these stories, you will discover that it is not a daunting exercise, and you do not need unlimited resources in order to give of yourself. And the reward for this discovery is invaluable. Finding purpose as I approach the second half of my life has been a comfort and joy, and I hope it will be for you as well.

—Susan Dixon, June 2022

ACKNOWLEDGMENTS

I want to acknowledge those responsible for helping to make this book a reality.

Bridget Soden Mills, Principal + Creative Director of Creative Vortex, Inc. for the cover design.

Patricia "Trish" Beaulieu for editing and publishing guidance, and Nancy Ratkiewich for layout and production.

Patti Larson, Founder and CEO of SunUp Group, Inc. who for several years now been a close confidant, colleague, partner, and friend. She also has been the guiding light in developing my voice and brand for all that I try to contribute.

Dita Shemke, Business Leader and my fiancée, for inspiring me to give of myself more fully in helping others and for loving me through the ups and downs of the past several years as I worked to create meaning in my life.

Most importantly, Susan Dixon, who has been a mentor, colleague, volunteer leader, and close friend. She more than anyone else has encouraged me to pursue my purpose with passion and dedication, and has kept me on the right path to be able to contribute my most cherished thoughts in a meaningful way.

INTRODUCTION

In 2016 I wrote *Redefining Retirement: Finding Purpose and Passion in Your Second Half* to focus on the great disappointment many feel when they follow the traditional retirement path of focusing mainly on leisurely activities during this significant time of life. As I described, a better alternative for many leaving the business world can be found in giving of themselves to help others. Some of us believe we don't need to wait until retirement to pursue purpose and passion. And many of us don't even want to retire, preferring to continue our business roles indefinitely. But again, incorporating purpose and giving into our daily (business) lives can greatly enhance the quality of life as we continue to grow and evolve.

However—and, whenever we reach this perspective, experiencing the many rewards that are the product of helping others learn, grow, and thrive is what I refer to as *"living a richer life."* My mission is to help more people "live richer lives," whatever that might look like. I recognize that business and family life certainly can be rewarding in many ways, but rarely do I find that most people's current focus is centered on their ultimate purpose in life, what they are passionate about, and how they want to leave society a bit better. They may be doing a great job of caring for their personal needs (for safety, security, shelter, food, etc.), but that is better described as survival rather than real fulfillment. I believe it is when we shift some of our focus and efforts from satisfying our own needs/wants to helping others that we find real purpose and fulfillment. Borrowing the phrase made popular by Bob Buford in his book *Halftime,* this shift in focus is the first step in turning personal success into lasting significance.

So, when I use the term *"living a richer life,"* I mean focusing one's efforts on helping others in a manner that fulfills you personally, professionally, and emotionally. There are countless ways in which this notion can be realized, and each of us has the opportunity to determine what this looks like, whom we help, how we help, and how much of our effort will be invested in this pursuit. But when we are in the zone where we are reaping great personal rewards because of the impact we are having on others, I believe it's fair to say we are living a much richer life.

I also believe that you don't have to be Bill Gates, a CEO, or run a Fortune 500 company to live this richer life as we all have something we can contribute (time, talent, or treasure). **We just need to be willing to consider how we can help others learn, grow, and thrive.** Are you ready for that next step in your personal journey toward living a much richer life?

To help you consider your future, this book focuses on the many diverse ways that people - young, old, and in between—have discovered the great rewards that come from helping others grow and prosper. I have attempted to share the personal stories of many of my friends, people who want more from life, and have found ways in which they can shift their focus, some in small ways and some in huge ways, to helping others. They are as different as you'll find, but they all share the common experience of *living a richer life.* It has been a pleasure getting to know these generous people and their journeys of discovery and fulfillment. I am inspired to follow their examples, and I hope you will be similarly inspired. Enjoy!

CHAPTER ONE

VOLUNTEERS AND VOLUNTEER LEADERS

The most common way that people find the rewards of helping others is through volunteering. This giving of time, and talent, is a critical ingredient in allowing non-profits to accomplish their missions. But it is also incredibly rewarding to those who experience firsthand the joys of shifting their focus from pursuing only their own needs and desires to that of helping others learn, grow, and thrive. This pursuit creates an important new sense of purpose that can help the giver continue his own personal growth at any point in life. A few of these volunteers become Volunteer Leaders, further engaging with an important cause and making an even bigger impact. This section explores the personal stories of these volunteers and volunteer leaders.

Matt O'Connell

I thought I was going to retire from the company. In my twenty years at the firm, I had moved from an entry-level sales rep position to leading our corporate divisions in Latin America, Europe, North America, and finally, the global team. During those years, we quadrupled revenue and became the most profitable division in the company. I loved it, and I couldn't imagine the company surviving without me, or more truthfully, me surviving without the company. Yet, despite the best-laid plans, all good runs do come to an end. We were acquired, and although it seemed very positive initially, things began to change. Leadership changes, consolidations, new synergies, and a new culture. During the transition, I went from being one of the most valuable members of the team to one of the "old guards," and slowly but surely, I realized that my best days at the company were behind me. It was time.

The company asked me to stay on as a consultant for twelve months which was financially attractive and would take up a few hours a week. The rest of the time was mine, and the thought of all that free time was terrifying. I had not had any free time in twenty years; my days were filled with meetings, conference calls, financial reviews, and travel. I had no idea how to fill my day without the imperatives of the business driving my schedule. This mid-career crisis led me to an exploration that proved to be one of the most valuable experiences of my life. I challenged myself to find purpose, meaning, and impact outside my corporate comfort zone. I needed to answer the question of how I could use the skills and talents that I have gained over the years to impact the world in a new way.

This exploration leads me to Haiti. Like many, I was horrified by the loss and destruction caused by the earthquake in Port au Prince in 2010. I am not sure why, but I decided I wanted to see if I could use my time to help alleviate some of the reigning desperation in Port au Prince. I met with an organization based in Los Angeles called J/P HRO. The organization assisted the tens of thousands of Haitians living in displacement camps after the quake. I offered to help in any way possible, and the JP team invited me to visit the camps to explore that opportunity.

During my second day in Port au Prince, I went to tour the largest of the displacement camps that were serving close to 60,000 people. JP HRO had set up a medical and dental clinic in the camp, and the dental clinic caught my eye. The clinic was very crude by our U.S. standards. The equipment was very rudimentary but was sufficient to pull teeth and alleviate the pain when there was no other option. I knew right away that I could help. I had spent twenty years in the dental manufacturing business, and I knew that we could access better equipment and materials to provide better care and health to people in the camp.

"I realized that I was getting more than I was giving in this project. My work in Haiti had become an essential part of my life."

Right then, I began my work with JP HRO. Our goal was to provide high-quality and safe basic dental care services to the people of the camp. I decide to spend the better part of my year off in Port au Prince toward realizing that goal. That year proved to be the most rewarding of my life. I had the privilege of working with the extraordinary JP HRO staff and a group of inspired Haitian dentists to build one of the best community dental clinics in Haiti.

My initial plan was to invest my year in helping build the clinic and then return to work when my consultancy was up. I did go back to work, but I did not leave Haiti far behind. I couldn't. I realized that I was getting more than I was giving in this project. My work in Haiti had become an essential part of my life.

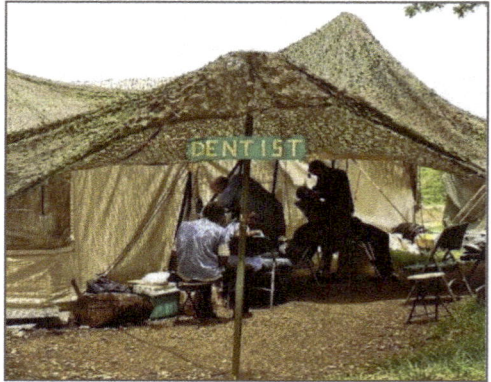

JP HRO Dental Clinic 2010

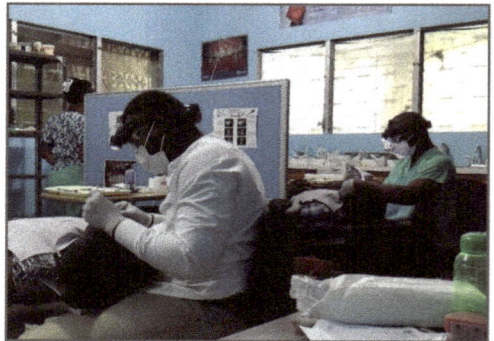

JP HRO Dental Clinic 2016

In the five years since returning to full-time work, I still am very involved in the work of our clinic. Over the years, we moved the clinic out of the camp and into the general community. We have hired three full-time Haitian dentists that provide free and safe care to over 8,000 patients per year who would otherwise not receive care. Next year, we will be adding one more dentist to our practice to service an additional 2,000 patients.

My year in Haiti showed me that my life is bigger than my business. I learned that I could have an impact that goes beyond the P&L of the company. During my year in Haiti, I found a mission and purpose that will be part of me for the rest of my life. Richard Ward and the team at Stifel are part of this mission with me. Sustain the work we began in Haiti and securing its long-term impact is the primary topic of our financial planning. My plan now is not to simply retire well. I plan to transition to continuing the work that has been so meaningful to me.

Michael Vaughn

First, I was curious. Then I was inspired.

My daughter had married a young man, an officer in the U.S. Marine Corps, based at the time at Camp Lejeune, North Carolina. Way over there on the other side of the Country. My Southern California hometown, the City of Rancho Santa Margarita (RSM), had "adopted" an infantry battalion, the 2nd Battalion, 5th Marines (the "2/5"), based at Camp Pendleton, California. And I learned of a local organization, Operation Help-a-Hero (OHH), doing some wonderful things to support the Marines, including the 2/5. I was curious because I had no idea how my daughter's life might evolve, married to an officer in the Marines. Curious about the way a father should be. So, I reached out to the group's leader, Cindy Farnum, and asked how I could help. Cindy Farnum had been my son's teacher in Elementary School and, by the way, was married to a Marine who had served as Commanding Officer of the 2/5. Cindy's response was simple and effective. Come on down to Camp Pendleton, she said—the 2/5 is coming home. From a long, tough deployment in Afghanistan. Tonight.

So, I drove down to Camp Pendleton, curious, and worked with the OHH volunteers to entertain and feed the Marines' families on the Parade Deck, waiting, for a few hours, for those white buses to arrive. The Marines of the 2/5 were coming home. From Afghanistan. Where they had been for about 10 months. In combat. Some of the Marines of the 2/5 did not make it home from this deployment, having given the ultimate sacrifice on foreign soil. Others made it home, but not in one piece. The buses did arrive after midnight. And when the Marines got off the busses and were dismissed by their company commanders, they quickly separated into two groups. Some were embraced with hugs and kisses of wives or girlfriends, with proud and relieved smiles of their mothers, fathers, kids, friends,

" And that all of us can learn a thing or two about serving with honor, courage, and commitment. Like they do. That inspired me. "

and family. A homecoming to remember. The others, the single Marines without family or friends on the Parade Deck, quickly made their way to the barracks. Because that was where they had a bed.

Now, no story involving the 2/5 is complete without mentioning two things. First, the 2nd Battalion, 5th Marines is the most decorated infantry battalion in the history of the U.S. Marine Corps. Second, the 2/5's motto, "Retreat, Hell!" comes from the French trenches of World War I, when a Marine officer was advised by a French officer to retreat. His reply? "Retreat? Hell, we just got here!"

So, there I was, on a Parade Deck at Camp Pendleton after midnight, greeting Marines, shaking their hands, welcoming them home, when I tried to engage in conversation with a young Marine. After introducing myself, welcoming him home, and explaining that I was here as a volunteer from the City of Rancho Santa Margarita, the young Marine had a question. A simple question. But in the circumstances, an extraordinary request. After 10 months or so of combat in Afghanistan, with a heavy rucksack on his back, eager to get to the barracks, the Marine had a question. He asked if he could bring a few of his buddies up to Rancho Santa Margarita. To do some community service. A project. Anything. Something to serve our community.

This is what a combat-fatigued Marine had on his mind at that moment, and he was serious about it. It occurred to me right then, right there, that the Marines know a thing or two about service. And that all of us can learn a thing or two about serving with honor, courage, and commitment. Like they do. That inspired me. It inspired me to do something. To do more. It didn't matter what it was if it was supporting Marines. That I could find some more time, some more energy, and some more desire to provide support to the Marines and families of the 2nd Battalion, 5th Marines.

Team 2/5 RSM was established in 2013 as a non-profit organization in Rancho Santa Margarita to provide support to the Marines and families of the 2/5 and to enhance the City's adoptive relationship with the 2/5.

My wife, Debbie, and I, and a small group of Team 2/5 RSM volunteers have supported the Marines and families of the 2/5 for over eight years. We provide volunteers for the 2/5's Family Readiness Team at events and programs on base at Camp Pendleton, at homecoming ceremonies, deployments, holiday parties, family days, and the like. And we bring Marines into RSM to engage in our community's events, including Patriot Day and Summer Concerts in the Park, where they can interact with residents of their adoptive hometown.

Among the most rewarding elements of my work with the 2/5 is the Unit's annual holiday party. Most of the time, the party is held when the Marines are deployed overseas in some far corner of the planet. The 2/5's Family Readiness Team invites me to play (rather, be) Santa Claus for the unit's annual holiday party. The kids, as resilient and proud as their parents in their service, believe. They always do.

Curious and inspired.

I am a partner with Taylor English Duma LLP, an Atlanta-based law firm, working remotely from my Southern California home with a practice focused on corporate transactions. I served on the Rancho Santa Margarita City Council from 2014 to 2018 and served as the City's Mayor in 2018, served on the City's Planning Commission in 2013 and 2014, and continue to serve my community in other organizations, including service on the Boards of Directors of the RSM Chamber of Commerce, the South Orange County Economic Coalition, and his homeowner's association.

Bob Greenberg

As a long-time Orange County resident and now retired Financial Planner, I have been giving back for over 25 years.

My non-profit experience started when I was asked to help the Orange County American Heart Association's Planned Giving Council, which led to my becoming the Board Chairman. When I stepped down, I realized there was no training for volunteer leaders and started the Non-Profit President's Forum, providing quarterly learning sessions for the Presidents and Chairs of local non-profits. This was eventually absorbed by what became OneOC today.

"In 2011 I saw a TV show about homeless veterans and started a personal journey that continues today. "

I was on the Board of the Social Enterprise Institute and led a leadership forum helping non-profits run earned income programs. That group is now called the Academies for Social Enterprise.

Soon after, I was recruited by a friend and became the Founding President of Advisors in Philanthropy. That organization continues today as a key vehicle for helping advisors to engage their clients in helping others.

In 2011 I saw a TV show about homeless veterans and started a personal journey that continues today. I went to the Orange County Community Foundation (OCCF) and asked what was happening with local veterans, only to learn they didn't know! OCCF and I started inviting donors, veterans, and non-profits serving them to meet and learn together, and OCCF eventually decided to make veterans one of their strategic initiatives. They've since helped form the OC Veterans Collaborative, facilitating cooperation among the various veteran-serving non-profits, worked with the OC Real Estate Industry to raise funds for the non-profits, and distributed over $3.5 million to veteran charities by the end of 2018.

When I retired in 2016, I decided to use some of my free time to help veterans and joined the board of Strength in Support (SIS), the only organization in OC focused on providing mental health counseling to veterans and their families more directly. SIS served over 1,000 people in 2017. I currently serve as Board president.

Volunteering has brought me tremendous personal satisfaction as well as helping OC become healthier and a more welcoming place for veterans and their families.

David Elliott

RELATIONSHIP BUILDER AND CONNECTOR OF PEOPLE

The Story Yesterday

Music and sports have always been at the core of what intrigued me and what I participated in through high school into my college years at the University of Arizona.

A music major first, then switching to health and coaching. Quite different, but later in life, it was always about people in either field.

Simple goals coming out of college: teaching and coaching basketball. I was blessed to do both over different periods in my life. Looking back, this, along with my music career, has shaped what I believe and desire to accomplish today. In all my travels in life, it has come down to making a difference in all endeavors. In music, it was about performance with others in sharing a message of hope. In teaching, it was helping students achieve. Coaching was about molding a group of young men into a "TEAM" that worked together to achieve the goal of winning. There have been many accomplishments along that way that I have been blessed with, but most importantly, the lesson of RELATIONSHIPS and the importance of that.

It was at the age of 52 when I was going through a divorce that I realized that working with people and connecting with them was simply ME. Through my HALFTIME experience over three plus years, I developed a clarity of who, what, and why. It took me over three years to develop a mission statement that today is my guiding principle of why and what I do. I am a big believer that we need a purpose/mission statement.

I have been blessed to meet many great people over the years, especially in the past 16 years, through my work at Vanguard University and the Santa Ana Chamber of Commerce. These past years I have realized and integrated the principles of Relationship Building and Connecting. It is FUN!

The Story Today

I have been a 30-year plus community member of Orange County. Currently serving as President/CEO of the Santa Ana Chamber of Commerce serving the second largest city in Orange County (375,000 people). In 2016, I founded the INSTITUTE for Community Impact focuses on helping individuals and organizations impact their communities through the (7) Pillars for Influence: Arts and Entertainment, Business, Social Services, Faith Community, Education, Government, and Healthcare. I partnered with longtime friend Russ Williams (founder of the Passkeys Foundation) and placed the INSTITUTE into the Foundation as its major program.

"My passion is 'Just Do Good,' and you will make a difference."

Before coming to the chamber in the summer of 2010 I served as Associate Vice President for University Relations at Vanguard University where I served in several roles for over 15 years. In addition, I am president of David Elliott & Associates, Inc., a business development consulting firm serving for-profit and non-profit businesses and organizations. People say I am known throughout Orange County as a "Relationship Builder and Connector of People." I like that. My passion is "Just Do Good," and you will make a difference. It is always about the people you are surrounded by that make you successful and significant.

Personal Mission: Serving God as a Catalyst and Difference Maker by Building Relationships, Connecting People, and Being an Influence for Good.

I hold a BS in Education from the University of Arizona (Go CATS!) and a MA in Music from Azusa Pacific University (That's right!).

My core strengths include leadership, business development, marketing, fund development, coaching/mentoring, RELATIONSHIP BUILDING, and CONNECTING PEOPLE. All with a common-sense approach. "Who knows you and whom do you know."

John Guastaferro

I am an award-winning marketing executive, non-profit leader, and professional magician! That's right, beyond my career as the Executive Director of the Anaheim Community Foundation and my leadership with several philanthropic organizations, I am an internationally acclaimed author and magician. I have lectured and performed across nine countries and can often be seen headlining at the world-famous Magic Castle in Hollywood.

Each day, I focus on making the impossible . . . possible. When I connect with a donor to make a difference in a child's life, it is a magical moment. Likewise, when I bring smiles to audiences as a magician, it is also very magical. It is this viewpoint that has guided me on a path of success with purpose.

"Whether I'm building brands, advancing causes, or sharing the power of magic with others, it is my overarching mission to connect people to extraordinary moments."

With experience in magic and business, I have emerged as a sought-out keynote speaker and facilitator. I combine showmanship with leadership to captivate audiences in his keynotes, board retreats, and team training. I focus on helping organizations spark magic in three core areas for success—team, brand, and cause.

As an only child raised by a single mom, I was naturally drawn to art, magic, and music growing up. My upbringing also shaped me to be an empathetic leader. Before my role as Executive Director for the Anaheim Community Foundation, I spent 18 years on the executive team for the Anaheim Family YMCA. While there, I elevated branding and led the way to raise over $5 million in grants and contributed support. In recognition of my work, I received four national philanthropic communication awards from the North American YMCA Development Organization.

❝A philanthropist is a person who donates time, money, skills, or talent to help create a better world. Anyone can be a philanthropist, regardless of status or net worth.❞

I am very involved as a philanthropic leader in Orange County. In 2016, I received my Certified Fundraising Executive credential. I am a Board member with Anaheim Community Foundation and Orange County Advisors in Philanthropy. I have also advanced the work of numerous non-profit organizations as a Preferred Training Specialist with OneOC.

Regarding fundraising, I have a mantra: "Stewardship is the goal—fundraising is the outcome." Isn't this so true? Relationships are the pinnacle of philanthropy.When done right, it inspires action, mutual respect, and shared purpose.

I recall earlier this year when someone introduced me as a "philanthropist." It admittedly caught me off guard. I never considered myself to hold such a noble title. I have always viewed my role more as connecting with philanthropists—not being one. This inspired me to find this wonderful definition of philanthropy at Fidelity Charitable:

"A philanthropist is a person who donates time, money, skills, or talent to help create a better world. Anyone can be a philanthropist, regardless of status or net worth."

This opened my eyes to what it truly means to be a philanthropist. For any of us who give our time, skill, experience, or resources to create a better world, we can all stand proudly as philanthropists.

"Titles do not define us. The next time someone asks what you do for a living, try answering without a job title or company name. Focus on the benefit you bring to the world. It's a powerful and enlightening way to uncover the true magic you create."

Perhaps my greatest trick is finding time to be involved in the community. Beyond my daytime job, I rarely say no to helping fellow non-profits and service organizations. I also travel the world to lecture and perform magic. Above all, I am a family man, very active with my wife and two daughters. And I look after my mom who lives nearby.

"There comes a time when the more you do, the easier and more powerful things become. I love finding synergy and uncommon connections in all that I do. I often draw from my experience as a magician to help wow donors or enrich my role as a dad by instilling the importance of giving back."

I frame my approach to both business and magic through a "one-degree" lens. In 2010, I authored the book *One Degree,* giving salient examples of how small, pivotal refinements can lead to extraordinary impact. *One Degree* has gone on to sell internationally, currently available in four languages.

To learn more about my outlook on connecting people to the extraordinary, be sure to visit at **www.OneDegreeConnect.com.**

Colleen Richardson

Describing my volunteer involvements, I am now aware that my commitment to give community service was an exercise in good karma: volunteering gave me so much more of a return than the time and effort I gladly donated!

Throughout my career, I actively joined efforts with professional organizations to collaborate with colleagues focused on expediting successful endeavors. Assisting with extracurricular special projects and standing committee work soon transitioned to appointed and elected positions with state, regional, and national membership organizations. Those volunteer opportunities also repaid me with added skills and achievements, which in turn tapped me for state government advisory panels, and invitations to federally funded national healthcare workshops.

Along with my volunteer path, I also trained and volunteered to address tough people situations that might benefit from the comfort, awareness, and decision-making strategies to reduce or overcome personal harm. I became a night shift volunteer at a domestic violence shelter, with a particular effort to support the youngsters torn away from their familiar surroundings, friends, pets, close relatives, and even toys. When I relocated cross-country, I became the first volunteer at a secure, private, and confidential group home for pre-and elementary school-age boys placed there by the court. Later, my husband and I volunteered at Ronald McDonald House, providing warm support for families of seriously ill children who need a quiet break to refresh— or an overnight room—while staying close to their fragile children.

Now that my schedule is free from extensive career obligations, I contribute my energy, abilities, and time to meaningful endeavors at other area non-profit organizations. At 2-1-1 Orange County, my tasks have included standardizing and updating health and medical entries in the Information and Referral (I&R) database, reaching out to the 100 domestic violence programs to assure the database and the countywide coalition have accurate quarterly updates and conducting a key leaders' assessment to identify our region's most relevant challenges and ways the newly merged 2-1-1 could harness its resources to solve them. As a OneOC team member, I have shared tactics for efficient membership renewal processes, been the point person to link trained volunteers willing to commit at the Board level with area non-profits currently recruiting specific capabilities for their boards of directors, and optimized the accuracy and consistency of OneOC's customer data records.

"... volunteering gave me so much more of a return than the time and effort I gladly donated! "

Volunteering is a continuing core value to me. Besides assisting my community and those in vital need—the prime reasons I share my time—I realize that I, too, am better for the experience.

Being a volunteer:

- provides purpose

- keeps me learning and mentally stimulated

- connects me with good people and strengthens ties to my community

- maintains my thinking and relationship skills

- brings pleasure and sparkle, even on gloomy days

I encourage everyone to share time and talent: identify your goals and interests, and then enjoy the gift of giving!

Charlie Hedges

I n 2017 my life was changed forever. I went to Uganda with Wells of Life—a charity that has provided access to clean water to more than 600,000 people in the most rural populations in Uganda.

It was there I got to see face-to-face the nearly inexpressible joy of children and parents who had recently received the gift of clean water!

The people we are privileged to serve in Uganda are among the poorest of the poor—no electricity, no toilets, no running water, no sinks or stoves, and only dirt for floors. But they are still among the happiest and most grateful people I have ever met.

"All my life experiences—advancing personal and corporate development, working with teams, and contributing my gifts—have resulted in the most significant time of my life."

Within months of that experience, in retirement, I joined the Board of Directors as Vice President. When I told my son, a catcher for the Cleveland Indians, what I was up to, he became an Ambassador for Wells of Life so that he too, might serve the needs of the poor in Uganda.

I have come to realize that I don't serve a charity. I serve communities of people without access to clean water and without the quality of life that comes with clean water and hands-on training in sanitation and hygiene.

In 2019, in addition to more than 100 new and restored water wells, we piloted a Healthy Village Program specifically designed for 2,257 households and more than 12,000 people.

Results were greatly inspiring:

- An 89% increase in access to clean water

- A 67% increase in latrine coverage

- A 79% improvement in the use of clean containers to transport water from wells to homes

- A 37% decrease in infant diarrhea

Yes, in 2019 alone, we saved the lives of hundreds (or thousands) and vastly improved the quality of life for tens of thousands.

I believe this is the work of God in my life. All my life experiences—advancing personal and corporate development, working with teams, and contributing my gifts—have resulted in the most significant time of my life. I get to fulfill the purpose of life as Aristotle wrote to "contribute to the value of society."

Yes, there truly comes a time in life when we advance from "success to significance."

I am a retired Executive Business Coach or "Partner in Thought" with CEOs of very large corporations. In addition, I coached Youth Baseball for nearly a decade.

Sue Koch

I spent most of my career in the Engineering and Construction industry. My career chose me more than I chose it. I started as a data entry processor, knowing from the beginning that I wanted to learn, grow, and become something more. I just didn't have a clue about who that might be.

I was ambitious enough to jump at new opportunities. I was primarily motivated by the desire to make more money than most women were able to make in those days. Eventually, I progressed to a Project Management position. In the beginning, I was attracted by making good money and by the opportunity to work on a variety of projects, travel around, and live in different places.

"My dream of making a career change suddenly felt like a nightmare."

But after years of doing that, the glamor wore off. All I wanted to do was stay in one place. I had grown weary of fighting the "good ol' boy" culture prevalent in the Engineering and Construction industry. Having to prove myself over and over again on each new project became exhausting.

I often toyed with the idea of making a career transition. It seemed like an impossible dream, and yet every time I heard someone who had left the company declare that it was the best thing they ever did, I yearned for the courage to go. One should be careful about what one wishes for. As John Lennon said, life is what happens when we are busy making other plans.

One day, seemingly out of the blue, the unthinkable happened. I was "invited" to take "early retirement." My dream of making a career change suddenly felt like a nightmare. My safe and comfortable life was being demolished with no new life to move into. What the heck was I supposed to do now?

Looking back, I believe the Universe puts events in motion for our evolution even before we consciously know that a life or career transition is necessary. I would likely never have made such a daunting move on my own.

Several things stopped me:

- I had been in my current career for so long that making a change was scary

- I didn't know what else I could do that would pay as well as my current job

- I was tired. I didn't think I had the energy to start over.

As awful and intimidating as it feels, there's a lot to be said about having no choice. My layoff forced me to do a ton of soul searching to discover what I wanted to do next. I had plenty of time for that since my layoff occurred a few months after September 11th, when no one was hiring. By taking my time and with the support of friends and colleagues, I discovered something that made a huge difference. I discovered my purpose to celebrate life playfully and passionately.

My purpose is my guiding light. It guided me to launch my business as a Career and Life Design Coach. I was driven by a desire to help people who found themselves in a similar position of having many skills and the desire to stay engaged at any age but have been tossed aside, mostly because they are no longer young.

I call it designing your Sexy Second Act, which means inventing a lifestyle that inspires, fulfills, and rewards you. My purpose guided me to write the book *Sexy Second Act: Remodel Your Life with Passion, Purpose, and a Paycheck®*. Publishing my book fulfilled a lifelong dream of becoming an author. I intend to encourage others to go for their dreams playfully and passionately at any age or any stage.

Purpose becomes an organizing principle around which you will find that making life decisions becomes simple. You get a clear view of how to make better choices. You learn to eliminate the urgent for the important. These days, I find that even when I am scared, I am excited to keep going. I no longer worry about money; I'm doing fine making less. I'm no longer tired. Instead, I feel invigorated and fulfilled.

I won't pretend that following your purpose is the easiest path. I don't believe it's supposed to be because if it's always easy, you aren't growing. But for me, despite the challenges, it continues to be a fun and rewarding path.

Nowadays, I provide coaching and mentoring services to those looking to transition into a more purpose-driven life as I run my firm, 3 Squares Coaching and Consulting. I have also been involved in Women's Sage, helping women find their new futures.

Michael Kogutek

My story begins as an undergraduate student at the University of Wisconsin-Oshkosh. I came there with a basic understanding that one of my career goals was to make a difference and help other people. I was blessed to take a psychology course with Dr. Gordon Filmer-Bennett. I was a part-time instructor and worked as Chief Psychologist at Winnebago State Hospital. After the first class, I wanted to do what Gordon does. It was in my heart and soul. I changed my major to psychology and never looked back. Gordon mentored me all the way.

"On top of that, I am having a blast!! This is not about me but them. I hope that before I leave this life, I can give more than I have taken. "

I spent 33 years as a psychologist in private practice as well as some part-time teaching. I always got up in the morning eager to make a difference. I believe what Kahlil Gibran said in *The Prophet:* "Work is love made visible." I retired in 2012 and felt it was time to give back what gifts were given to me. I have volunteered at Second Harvest and South County Outreach. Since 2015, I have been involved in volunteer coaching with Executive Coaches of Orange

County (ECofOC). I am the Past Chair of the organization. The mission of helping non-profit managers realize their goals and leadership potential speaks to me. It aligns with my skill set.

On top of that, I am having a blast!! This is not about me but them. I hope that before I leave this life, I can give more than I have taken.

Julie Cho

I am the principal attorney of Cho Law Firm, APC. I am an estate planning attorney with over 23 years of legal experience and have counseled individuals in matters involving estate planning, wills and trusts, and business planning.

After having worked in large law firms at the beginning of my legal career, I realized that the best means to provide the personalized service I believe all clients deserve from large corporations to single parents—was to open my practice in the city where I was raised. While possessing extensive experience in business litigation and business law, I have a passion for estate planning and providing peace of mind to families.

"I seek to be a positive example to my two young children . . . ," The driving force behind my work is community education and service. I meet this goal by providing educational seminars and consultations within my community on the benefit of trusts, probate avoidance, and succession planning. I especially like to empower the special needs community by advising them on the benefits of a special needs trust and the need to protect government benefits for their loved ones.

Furthermore, I am involved in various philanthropic organizations in Orange County. I serve in the Pacific Coast

Exchange Club, which serves to honor and help local veterans, and I work with the Child Abuse Prevention Center helping to strengthen families and prevent child abuse. Furthermore, I support the Free Wheelchair Mission, a humanitarian and faith-based non-profit that manufactures and delivers cost-efficient wheelchairs to developing countries worldwide.

I transcend my practice beyond mere document preparation by becoming connected to my clients and their lives. I bring a personalized approach to each client's unique estate planning needs.

I grew up in Irvine, attended UCLA for undergraduate studies, and obtained my law degree from the University of Illinois at Urbana-Champaign law school. I seek to be a positive example to my two young children, one of whom (a 12-year-old!) desires to serve her country as a Navy Fighter Pilot.

Marla Noel

I have a long and distinguished business history. Trained as a CPA, I began my career as an accountant aiming to run my firm. I shifted gears and pursued a career in corporate America, working for May Co., Seely Wolf, and finally, Fairhaven Memorial Park and Mortuary. I rose to the President's position.

I continued my personal growth with an MBA from Chapman University. I was active with Vistage and Women Presidents' Organization and learned firsthand how strategic planning could help organizations.

I served on many non-profit boards, including OCARC, the Boys & Girls Club of Central Orange Coast, Alzheimer's Association, Orange County, Woman Sage, and ICCFA. I served as president of the Santa Ana Rotary Club and was responsible for Santa Ana Rotary Club's involvement in the Interact Club at Saddleback High School, Rebuilding Together, and Corazon de Vida. I also joined the Irvine Rotary Club for many years. I ran the Fairhaven Board and managed the Board of another private entity.

> **"My second-half focus is to help more people enjoy what they're doing with their lives."**

My long-range, forward-thinking led to Fairhaven being acquired by a $3-billion-dollar company in 2015, creating significant wealth for the owners and key employees of the company. I stayed on after the acquisition closed to ensure smooth management and employee transition but knew I would need new challenges for the years ahead. My search for a new direction ended with establishing OC Growth Advisors, which serves businesses by helping them improve business focus and institute good general business practices through creative one-on-one sessions with the business owner and key employees. I am also a chair for WPO, Women President's Organization, a peer group for business owners.

My second-half focus is to help more people enjoy what they're doing with their lives. I will continue my work with OC Growth Advisors and the Women President's Organization. I enjoy the challenges that come from using my skills and experiences to impact the community.

Shawn Wehan

I live a life of purpose, which, in my case, is to help bridge the gap between the needs of the community and the gifts and talents of its members. As I put it, "The world is full of people who want to be a force for good. They sometimes just don't know where to start."

My story begins my freshman year of college when I interned at a soup kitchen and homeless shelter located in the heart of Denver, Colorado. Every day I would mop the shelter floors and spend time interacting with community members, learning their stories and struggles. I found the work fulfilling and even more enjoyable than my time studying radio broadcasting. Over the years, I volunteered for numerous community organizations, and upon graduating from college, I left radio altogether and joined the Jesuit Volunteer Corps for a year of service work in Mobile, Alabama.

At 22, I returned to my hometown of Dana Point, California, and began a career as a youth minister. For ten years, I introduced thousands of teens to the value and joy of community service work. My programs included numerous trips to orphanages in Mexico and assisting non-profits throughout Orange County. As I often share, "I like to pull people out of their comfort zone and watch their surprise when they discover how good it feels to use their gifts and talents in service to others."

In 2009, I formed a non-profit called Future Leaders of Our Community (FLOC), a young professional organization focused on awareness and hands-on volunteering with local non-profits. I grew the organization throughout San Diego, Orange County, and Los Angeles, working with hundreds of non-profits and thousands of young professionals. It was during this time that technology and smartphones began to present a new opportunity for engagement with non-profits. I envisioned a world where one could use a smartphone to connect with a non-profit that meant something to them and then make donations, purchase tickets, and request to volunteer, all with just a few easy clicks. I saw this technology as an extraordinary opportunity to democratize philanthropy.

"The world is full of people who want to be a force for good. They sometimes just don't know where to start. "

In 2013, I co-founded, Givsum, Inc. (short for "Giving Summary") to bring all elements of philanthropy (donors, non-profits, service clubs, schools, and businesses) onto a single platform where they can all interact. My team and I designed Givsum so users could quickly find opportunities to engage in their community and by doing so build a philanthropic resume and earn a Givsum Score™. Over the last five years, the platform has steadily grown. It is working to expand the scope of philanthropy by encouraging users to actively share their profiles, which inspires further community engagement.

Along with being the CEO of Givsum, Inc., I am an Executive Coach with Emergent Success, LLC; the host of the podcast American Philanthropy and a member of the Advisory Team for the Institute for Community Impact.

I have devoted my life to building a more engaged and inspired community. Whether it be through hands-on service, ministry, non-profit leadership, or technology, I am committed to helping others find their "greater purpose." While I have already done so much in that regard, I am just getting started and know that our collective future will be far brighter than any of us can individually imagine.

Bill Cunningham

I am from the rural Midwest. My small-town high school graduating class was only 36 students. I pride myself on that upbringing of traditional values, which gave me an innate service heart. My father, Bill Sr., expected that every driveway of a senior citizen in the neighborhood is shoveled by his six sons and sometimes the three daughters without expecting a reward.

I launched my adult life adventure in the United States Coast Guard. I served in various posts, including that of a lighthouse crew for offshore lights in Southern Maine. As part of an inspection team, I found that flying out to the lights was especially exciting and

> **"I have had a life-long passion for serving my country, community, and veterans' organizations."**

harrowing at times. I found the solitude of the keeper and my typically young family interesting and, at times, awe-inspiring.

My favorite duty was being part of the permanent crew aboard the USCG Barque Eagle, a tall ship stationed at the Coast Guard Academy, where I learned 17th-century sailing techniques. In addition to my regular shipboard duties, I worked some 15-stories aloft in the rigging, at times in heavy North Atlantic seas. Later I continued to enjoy the challenges of being a professional tall ship sailor and was named Commodore of Friends of Argus in Newport Beach some years ago.

After leaving the Coast Guard, I had a satisfying 35-year career as a nationally Certified Paralegal, often being asked to mediate complex cases. I learned that conflicts could often be broken down into a fundamental misunderstanding that unfortunately ballooned into litigation—finding and resolving that initial rift often resulted in resolution.

Today I am a Council-certified Emergency Operations Professional and the CEO and Developer of BERT Workplace Safety Solutions, an organization devoted to OSHA compliance and FEMA principles, saving life and limb by alleviating fear. There is no greater reward than to receive testimonials of how injury rates have decreased at the client's high-hazard facility or how an individual has helped in a crisis with poise and resolve.

I have had a life-long passion for serving my country, community, and veterans' organizations. I currently advocate and assist veteran entrepreneurs in guiding veteran business and service-disabled business owners to take their ventures to the next level. I have also recently volunteered for the Veterans Outpost at the Orange County Veteran and Military Family Collaborative.

In addition to my veteran's work, I serve on the Executive Committee and board of directors for Leadership Tomorrow OC and am active at my church which meets at the Newport Sea Base of the Boy Scouts of America.

I live with my wife, Holly, in Orange, California, and enjoy being a dad to my grown children and granddad to my growing number of active grandchildren.

Traci Shirachi

I am the CEO of The Mark USA, Inc. The Mark helps non-profits, businesses, and academic organizations collect, analyze, and visualize data; manage projects and programs; streamline strategic plans; monitor progress; evaluate impact; maintain compliance; and report results to stakeholders and funders.

I am responsible for making key business decisions to increase The Mark's abilities to address client needs. I work with the evaluators within the organization to deliver quality client service. At the heart of my work at The Mark and everything I do, is to help others and make a difference; this is my essence and purpose.

I have over 17 years of work experience with consulting companies of various sizes, including PricewaterhouseCoopers. I earned an M.B.A. from Vanderbilt University.

At the heart of my work at The Mark and everything I do, is to help others and make a difference; this is my essence

> **"I believe that it is only when we are a hero to someone and others that we find meaning, significance, and indeed the depth of our soul that is the essence of man (or woman) kind."**

and purpose. I do this by helping organizations to get very clear on their achieved outcomes and measuring those outcomes to allocate resources better and demonstrate systematic change to funders and key stakeholders, thus allowing them to do more good work.

As a working mom, I am a living example of a hero to my young kids, teaching them what a life well-lived looks like and how to have the tools to be successful in life. I desire to be a role model to them and others about what it means to be a part of positive change. This extends beyond my family and applies to the broader community here in Orange County, Southern California, and beyond. I believe that it is only when we are a hero to someone and others that we find meaning, significance, and indeed the depth of our soul that is the essence of man (or woman) kind.

Key Takeaways from Volunteers and Volunteer Leaders

I'm just amazed at all the ways that these volunteers have found to participate in the great endeavor of helping our vibrant non-profit community. For some, it has been a natural extension of their work or business. For others, their involvement had morphed over time into something much greater than when they began. And for a few, they have found ways to lead and direct other volunteers in a great collaboration worth so much more than individual efforts usually are. I'm inspired by the countless hours these people have invested, the impact they've made, and most importantly, how fulfilled, they feel when they devote their efforts to helping others learn, grow, and thrive.

CHAPTER TWO

VOLUNTEERS/ PHILANTHROPISTS

Often, volunteers get even more engaged with the causes that inspire them. They want to contribute to the mission beyond what they might solely by donating their labor. They contribute both time and treasure to their favorite organizations, also filling the role of "philanthropist." Others support important causes through their financial donations, usually starting small and growing their gifts sometimes quite significantly to the non-profits addressing their most important issues. Such gifts are usually cash but may also include securities, real estate, business interests, retirement account assets, life insurance, and other assets. Large and small, current or deferred, these contributions are the essence of philanthropy, a critical aspect of American life and success. And a few unique people go even further in their philanthropic efforts. They commit their business or the profits from their business to support a favorite cause, earning them the title of Social Entrepreneur. While all featured in this section qualify as Philanthropists, I wonder if you can find the Social Entrepreneurs in the group.

Charles Antis

I want to live life for my purpose, which is to help ignite the passion for a personal cause in everyone. But I didn't always feel that way. At age 19, as a student at BYU in Utah, I went on a traditional Mormon mission to Thailand. Uncomfortable about pushing my family's religion over Buddhism, I struggled to find fulfillment.

But one day, at a local orphanage, my life changed when a crippled 9-year-old gestured for me to pick her up. After holding her for a few minutes, I noticed that every time I started to put her down, the deeper she pushed her hands into my torso, as she did not want to be put down.

"My motto has become, 'the more we give, the more we grow,' and business has grown dramatically for me over the past decade."

The more I held her, the deeper the feeling of connection, of purpose, grew in me. In the end, I held the child for more than four hours. I learned that day that helping others is the key to personal fulfillment. I returned from my mission and went into the business world and started my own business, Antis Roofing and Waterproofing, in 1989.

I became quite proficient at fixing leaky roofs, and the word got around. I got a call from a family needing help with a leaky roof. When I drove out to find the home, I noticed that not only was there mold in the home but there was also mold in the old mattresses the family used. Conditions had worsened because the family could not afford to repair their failing roof. I scraped together some roofing materials and fixed the roof for free. The experience led him to adopt his company's mission, which is to keep families safe and dry.

It also led me to the Orange County chapter of Habitat for Humanity, to which I began donating in 2009. Since then, my firm has donated every roof for all Habitat for Humanity homes built in Orange County – some 70 homes. My motto has become, "the more we give, the more we grow," and business has grown dramatically for me over the past decade.

I enjoyed this experience so much that I encouraged the National Roofing Contractors Association to adopt the Ronald McDonald Houses as their national charity partner, and the association's non-profit arm, The Roofing Alliance, is now ramping up to donate all roofing needs for the organization nationwide and in Canada.

At this point, I am driven by the goal of creating a better world to live in and believe the business world has a big role to play. I leverage my relationships with the U.S. Chamber of Commerce and others to show businesses that they must adopt responsible methods of participating in their communities if they want to survive and thrive. I fully believe that adopting a cause is how to best help all stakeholders in a business. As I put it, "put purpose before profit," which I see as the source of doing good every day.

Canon Douglas Edwards

Success with Purpose: Establishing a Big Hairy Audacious Goal

When Richard Ward approached me to write a column about myself for **successwithpurpose.org,** I was flattered, amused, and hesitant. Richard has been my financial advisor for four decades and my BFF for nearly half a century. There was no way I could say, "No, thank you." And so, I write.

Since early childhood, I knew I would be an Episcopal priest, a US Senator, or a Supreme Court justice. At age 20, I looked under the hood of politics and scratched the goal of being a Senator.

I was a very successful collegiate debater and public speaker, winning national awards. Law school and the path to the Supreme Court were there. I love constitutional law to this day and would gladly accept an appointment to the Supreme Court (watch out, Citizen's United!), but the phone call has yet to come.

The call that came loud, clear, and repeatedly was to be ordained as an Episcopal priest happened in 1984. I suppose the rest of my life has been a feeble attempt to be faithful to this calling filled with purpose. Success for a priest has a very success is as much attributable to the values ingrained in parish ministry.

Episcopal clergy is encouraged to develop for themselves a personal BHAG, a "Big Hairy Audacious Goal." The concept comes from the Harvard Business School and is intended to differentiate companies with intergenerational success from the 99.9 percent of companies that rise and fall like blades of grass.

A proper BHAG requires that you do NOT have the resources available or the means to acquire the resources to achieve your Big Hairy Audacious Goal. It requires the ability to look over the horizon and imagine what lies ahead. This certainly applied to me. With a salary of $28,000 and no inherited wealth, I had no financial means to achieve any goals involving money. But I did have the social capital of Church and family to support my vision, and this was invaluable to keep alive the spark. It would take more than a decade before I made my first visit to Ghana, West Africa.

My BHAG emerged from a series of dreams while studying the life story of Albert Schweitzer as part of preparing a sermon. In my dreams, I was told to help Africa. I embraced these dreams as a message from the Almighty and began a quest with this purpose. It took almost 10 years to visit Ghana, West Africa, for the first time to formalize my BHAG while on a retreat. Once there, my call to "Help Africa" was crystallized, and my BHAG launched as I put to paper and a support group two specific goals: establish and fund a pension program for indigenous clergy in the rainforest of West Africa and bring safe sustainable drinking water to 250,000 souls.

As my commitment to Africa grew, I realized that while my parish endorsed my vision to help African villages and local priests living in extreme poverty (their wages were $100/year with no retirement!), the call to serve Africa was mine, not the parishes. To achieve my BHAG, I would need to find a way to make money, more money than I imagined I could ever do.

I started by establishing a foundation and opening myself to leaving full-time parish ministry for the world of business. Scary and exciting! The opportunity came in 2004 when I was offered to run a privately held utility that was in bankruptcy. Not a great prospect, uh? But it was. In addition to a sudden income of $100,000 (nearly unheard of for a parish priest), I ultimately received a controlling stake in the emerging company. Over the next 10 years, we grew the company from $2 million in revenue to almost $30 million and became quite profitable. It was not a straight-line growth chart. I went for a year without receiving any compensation during the Second Great Depression

> **" I've grown to embrace the African adage, 'If you want to go fast, go alone; if you want to go far, travel together.' "**

and was within days of losing everything before landing a large job, thanks to the Obama Administration's public works initiative. We weathered the recession and came back roaring. The company became my BHAG's primary funding source as I was able to pour over $2 million into African water projects, community development, and a clergy pension fund which was created out of thin air. I had crossed over the horizon and discerned the path to accomplish my charitable life goals.

I ultimately sold my controlling interest in the company and established a charitable trust so that my personal needs were met in my lifetime, and the BHAG would have the needed financing in the next generation. Others who were part of this business venture established charitable trusts to support my BHAGs down the road. I've grown to embrace the African adage, "If you want to go fast, go alone; if you want to go far, travel together."

Having sold my business interest, I became restless and invested in more businesses. They are small today, what may be described as maintenance companies, but they still provide the funds to enable our projects to move forward.

Two thousand eighteen is the year my first BHAG reaches its milestone—the clergy pension scheme is fully funded for current clergy, and new clergy is now part of the country's social security system. Yes, this was a 20-year journey with many challenges that ultimately became a success. Who'd have thought?

I have a long way to go toward bringing water to 250,000 souls, but in large part, a new national public water program in Ghana has accomplished my goal. In 2021 three villages received safe drinking water. The goal is to drill wells for five remote villages annually until the BHAG is fulfilled.

The call to Help Africa continues to burn. In 2014 I took on a new BHAG, freeing 1,000 children from slavery in Ghana. Again, I haven't the resources, but for this BHAG, I am part of a wonderful team of volunteer abolitionists. In March 2018 we crossed the mark of 100 children rescued from slavery through our fundraising and work with a great Ghanaian NGO. In 2021 we reached 250 freed children. If we can match our vision to supporters with a million dollars, we will have the funds to realize our goal. I hope to realize this BHAG in my lifetime.

My life has always included a desire to make a difference in the world. The challenge has been identifying the specifics and the means required and then waiting on the moment. It is not passive waiting. It is waiting grounded in St. Augustine's admonition, "Pray as if everything depends upon God, and work as if everything depends upon you."

Nurtured by family and friends, I am as busy though it is my own making. I play golf, spend time with grandchildren, and recently took on a part-time voluntary gig as the Episcopal Chaplain at a large university. I spend more and more time with medical professionals as my body reminds me that we are mortal, and I am beginning the winter of my days on earth. Simply put, I work for Africa, attempting to succeed in business so that I might achieve my BHAGS. I suspect it will always be thus for as long as God grants me vision and breath.

In the words of Dag Hammarskjold, "For all that has been, 'Thank you.' For all that is yet to come, 'Yes!'"

Donnie Crevier

I am on a mission to help kids who need and want a hand up. I reveal that this impetus is rooted in my childhood. Despite growing up in the affluent community of Laguna Beach, I remember the many challenges my single mother faced. As they moved from apartment to apartment, I found stability at the Boys & Girls Club of Laguna Beach—which I remain deeply connected as a member of its board of directors. I, of course, had a long successful career in the automobile industry and believed my involvement with local non-profits during those years helped make my business more successful as my employees were more fulfilled with their participation.

Ultimately, I sold the family auto dealership bearing my name and was able to give more time to help others, particularly kids, get started on the right path. "I'm especially focused on getting kids to think more about their education and getting them excited about learning and completing school," which I helped accomplish by providing scholarships to kids who come from disadvantaged homes.

I have a long history of supporting Orange County's non-profit community. I have served on the Orange County Human Relations Council, the Boys & Girls Club of Laguna Beach Board, the Laguna Beach Community Foundation Board, the Laguna Playhouse Board, and the Western Medical Center Board.

One of my most innovative philanthropic endeavors combines two of my greatest passions: youth education and the automotive industry. A partnership of the Santa Ana Chamber of Commerce and Santa Ana Unified School District, High School Inc. Academies (HSI) helps students develop the specific skills needed to work in high-growth, high-tech industries. I provided resources to kick-start HSI a decade ago, lending my support to train automotive technicians who would be "ready to hire" upon graduation from high school. Since

" I'm especially focused on getting kids to think more about their education and getting them excited about learning and completing school . . . . "

then, I, along with other HSI leaders, have realized we are doing more than simply preparing students for sustainable employment, which points to students' 97 percent high school graduation rate. "These kids develop a passion for learning," who also serves as HSI board chair this year. "They see the benefits of education in the long term."

I am a great example of finding and pursuing a greater purpose from my success, and our community is much stronger because of my efforts in so many ways for several years.

Victoria Collins

How Will Your Story be Told?

At this stage of my life, I think about the values, hopes, and dreams I most want to leave our children and grandchildren. How will my story be told and what will my legacy be?

It's clear to me that legacy is not about wealth but about your actions—how they will define you and how they will impact others. A legacy is something bigger than who you are today. It is more than you did this week, this month, or even this year. A legacy is something you are creating right now, whether you realize it or not.

This open letter to my eight grandchildren might be a good start:

"You've given me such joy as I've watched you grow from infants to toddlers to the young men and women you are now in college. The changes you've seen in your lifetime have happened at warp speed compared to those I saw when I was your age. It's hard for you to imagine that I was alive before computers, before iPhones, before Twitter, Facebook, and Google.

"My parents were good role models for me, as yours were for you, about the whole idea of philanthropy. I remember the little cardboard boxes we brought home from school to collect coins for needy families. When there was an opportunity to help others less fortunate, we did so as a family; it brought us together with feelings of gratefulness and purpose. We had a sense of responsibility and respect. We treated others with dignity and were grateful for the blessings we had.

"If I could give you two pieces of advice on philanthropy it would be to first be an engaged board or committee member. Writing a check is good, but sharing ideas, connections, and enthusiasm along with financial resources is even better; second, while the heart is important, use your mind and business skills in choosing non-profits to support. Do they produce measurable positive outcomes that can be documented?

"From each organization I've supported, I've learned more than I imagined and gained more than I've given. That will be true for you too."

"There will be a variety of worthy causes that call to you and what you want to support will also change over time. Over the years, I've supported many organizations, but they seem to have a common thread of empowering women and children with financial knowledge. Being involved with starting a microenterprise development fund for women, I learned that for the amount of money a good dinner costs in Newport Beach, I could help a woman buy a sewing machine to start her own business and support her family in Africa. Being involved with the American Heart Association, I learned the value of raising awareness for women and supporting research about women's heart health.

"Starting the Invest in Yourself Conference which later became WISE, I learned that when women have knowledge and confidence about their finances, nothing can stop them. Being on the Board of Human Options, I learned that it takes a team of wonderful, dedicated people to break the cycle of domestic violence and provide a place to heal and move forward. Being on the Board of United Way, I've learned that setting priorities and measurable goals are critical for addressing issues like homelessness in our community.

"From each organization I've supported, I've learned more than I imagined and gained more than I've given. That will be true for you too."

Lee Goldberg

I was born in The Bronx NY into an immigrant Jewish family that came through Ellis Island. As we say these days . . . that is how I "identify." Yet, it was important to, back then, and certainly in my family, to assimilate into, and thrive in, American society.

However, as part of that "assimilation" and rise into the mid-1900s average American middle-class included an edict that we should never forget who we were or where we came from. That edict required that you do what you can to help those still struggling and less fortunate than you. (I can't count how many times my grandmothers told me to eat everything on my plate because there were starving kids in Europe. It made no sense to me at the time . . . but the price for challenging my grandmothers was too high.)

"I think that's when it first started to hit me . . . maybe the everyday person really can make a difference. "

So, a charity in my mind as a kid was donating/raising money for charitable purposes and volunteering in charitable organizations. I watched my mother and grandmothers take leadership roles in various religious-based charitable entities. I watched as my father volunteered in financial leadership positions and sat on Boards at the synagogue. And of course, I raised money every Halloween (in a small tin can for UNICEF and got some candy too) and participated in food and clothing drives regularly as a kid in my parent's household. I never really had any passion for it. It was just expected of me.

When it came time to raise my own family, that expectation pervaded. My former spouse, a very well-respected lawyer herself, sat on the Boards for many years for several well-established charities including CCAP, CASA, and Mary's Shelter. I spent my time volunteering in the local youth sports leagues. And again, the family regularly participated in 5K walks, various fundraisers, and food and clothing drives. Then my daughter, while in high school, was one of the co-chairpersons of the first Aliso Viejo Relay for Life. I thought it was cute. They then raised more than $80,000 in 24 hours.

I think that's when it first started to hit me . . . maybe the everyday person really can make a difference. However, it was not until years later, when both of my kids left the house to start their own lives and careers (both dedicating their lives to the service of others in the healthcare industry—about which I am very proud), that I have the time, the resources, and frankly, the desire, to do a little bit more.

It started when a friend and client asked me to assist her with her dream to help the children of underserved communities. So, in 2015, I formed and continue to be a Board Member of, Necessities for Children (**www.necessitiesforchildren.org**). NFC is a registered 501(c)(3) organization whose mission is to support underserved children by enhancing and enabling computer science education, resulting in critical skill development, empowerment, and a better quality of life. Every child has the potential to change poverty in their community; NFC helps these children get started. This has become a passion.

Then the next year, another friend and client asked that I help him and his wife form an organization dedicated to protecting those who serve all of us—law enforcement officers. Most people do not know that not all police departments provide their officers with the necessary protective gear to be on the streets. Often, this leaves the officer (usually newly sworn) with the regrettable choice to provide for his/her family while going without protection. So, in 2016, I formed and continue to be a Board Member of E614 Corporation (**www.e614.org**). E614 is a 501(c)(3) charitable organization that provides Level III ballistic body armor at no cost to officers in need nationwide. To date, E614 has provided body armor to 934 officers but has a waitlist of over 4,500 officers in need. That's 4,500 LEOs whose lives are at daily unnecessary risk of lack of protective equipment. Again, this has become a passion to resolve.

Finally, I also give as much time and expertise as I can to my dear friend Antoinette Balta, the executive director of Veterans Legal Institute (**www.vetslegal.com**). VLI is a registered 501(c)(3) committed to assisting low-income veterans and their families at no cost with legal representation and administrative assistance regarding their rights, privileges, and government programs. Once again, my passion lies with this organization as these people have sacrificed so my family can live in a safe and free country, and yet, for the most part, they have been abandoned by our society.

My focus is now on helping with our local community's needs by supporting the people close to me and their causes. I feel that in supporting the charitable passions of my friends and clients, my world has become enhanced. However, I feel that my journey has just begun. I look forward to being present and actively involved when I see the need arise and where I can help. If you would like to know more about any of the above organizations, please do not hesitate to contact me—we would love to have you come aboard.

Leilani Quiray

Human Resources + Philanthropy—how does one do both? I found a way—by founding "be the change HR, Inc." Of course, it wasn't as easy as that since we all know building a business isn't for the weak of heart and neither are the trials and tribulations of life.

When I launched my company in October of 2017, I wrote a blog post entitled, "The Beginnings of be the change HR."

"Truth be told, I have it tattooed on my back, 'Be the change you wish to see in the world.'"

I've been doing HR since I was 16 years old when the neighbor wanted to hire me to do his payroll. My career since then has been a beautiful mix of hard work and opportunity. Throughout my HR career, I began volunteering at Working Wardrobes, coaching men and women who are transitioning back into the workforce from some type of difficult life situations: homelessness, abuse, addiction, sex trafficking, and veterans entering civilian life. I give blood, donate money, and feed and clothe the homeless.

But I wanted to do more.

I had been toying with the idea of a company that donated a percentage of the money it made to charity.

Companies who are not only "for-profit" but also companies who promise to always give back. Why couldn't I do it?! Why couldn't I build a company that promised to always give back? And that was the birth of "be the change HR, Inc."

Truth be told, I have it tattooed on my back, "Be the change you wish to see in the world." Overnight I built what I had been dreaming of. And seconds after I was able to launch, I got my first client. I am blessed. I am also out to change the world.

My dream . . . that I will influence others to be "conscious capitalists." That my company will grow into several consultants who believe in great work and the betterment of the world through their work

I don't think it'll be just a dream . . . it's going to happen.

So, to all our future clients, thank you for being part of this change. Together we can "be the change" and do some great HR work in the meantime!

And here we are, present day, in my second year of business.

What I failed to mention in my initial blog is there was a burning desire to help others because I had struggled immensely in my 20s. I had been like the clients I serviced in the non-profits I worked for. I had lost nearly everything and hit rock bottom myself. The minute I felt I was at a place both career-wise and health-wise I promised I'd give back to those in need. From that moment on I had such a passion for helping others.

I feel our responsibility is to lift others when they cannot lift themselves. If it weren't for the love of my family, friends, and strangers, I wouldn't have made it to where I am today. There is no way. And here I am with my hand outstretched to others to pull them up with me. It's a serious climb outta rock bottom.

It's one step in front of the other with a relentless drive to be "better" for yourself and those you love until you climb out of the hole and that is only the beginning. Then there is the trek to improve, do better, and strive for success. It's a long road, but we can all get there.

So, here is my "Why?" Because we all need a helping hand. We all have a story. We all need someone to turn to us and say, "Hey, look at me . . . you can do it too."

Oh, and what does my business do besides give back and have a kick-butt founder at the helm?

"be the change HR, Inc.," an Orange County-based conscious company and social enterprise, provides HR support for small-to-medium sized businesses in any facet of HR from pre-hire to post-term and everything else that happens in between. If it involves your employees, call us, and we can handle it. We make HR easy and change our little part of the world.

"Be the change you wish to see in the world." —M. Gandhi

Yup, we're doing just that!

Liza Krassner

I am a first-generation Filipino who came to California as a teenager and is currently an administrator at UCI's Program in Public Health. I love jazz. "It's important to me. It is America's original and greatest art form. It is diverse, unique, and encompasses almost everyone." I also enjoy the dance arts, especially the tango, which I dance socially whenever my time allows. "Jazz and tango are art forms built on improvisation." "It's just like life—we have to constantly improvise."

In 1997, I gave birth to a wonderful son who was later diagnosed with autism spectrum disorder (ASD). I later discovered that the tango had a tremendous impact on my understanding of the concept of connection through the movement of the dance.

> **"For me, this is impact. 'Art heals,' one experience, one life at a time. And that matters to this caregiver."**

The discovery was truly healing, and this learned concept of non-verbal communication or "connection" with another individual on the dance floor was brought home to train me on being more in tune with my son. This effect continues to be the driving force in my public service and philanthropic efforts in supporting the arts in promoting inclusive communities. "Art is essential." "It educates and informs, teaches appreciation and empathy, promotes cultural understanding, and builds community."

There is no doubt that the effect of the pandemic on the arts has been devastating. My thoughts are with the artists. "For many of us adjusting under quarantine, we continue to enjoy all the creative ways artists keep us entertained as they improvise in how they deliver their art to us. They give back, and so should we."

Public service, for me, centers on having an impact. I worked with the Irvine Barclay Theatre through their ARTSReach Program, partnering with the Regional Center of Orange County in bringing in persons with developmental disabilities to enjoy a pre-show sound check with Grammy Nominee Dr. Bobby Rodriguez. After the event, I was approached by a parent who shared that she was a musician who gave up music altogether because her daughter, who has autism, could not tolerate her playing her instrument at home. "Thank you for the sensory-friendly theater performance for the attendees. It is healing to hear live music again," she said. For me, this is impact. "Art heals," "one experience, one life at a time. And that matters to this caregiver."

I received my B.A. in Psychology from UC Irvine and completed my Master's in Public Administration at Cal State University at Long Beach. I currently serve as a Board member of the Regional Center of Orange County, the Center Club of Costa Mesa, and am a past Board member of the Irvine Barclay Theatre. I serve on two advisory Boards including the Irvine Residents with Disabilities Advisory Board and with KKJZ 88.1 FM, a public radio station broadcasting from Cal State Long Beach committed to the promoting of jazz. I currently live in Irvine with my husband and oldest son. My younger son is living in Washington, DC while in college, preparing for a life in public service.

Norris Battin

How To Retire Happy

Stan Hinden, a Washington Post business journalist, passed away recently at 90. In an obituary tweet, columnist David Ignatius wrote, "In addition to his column for [our Washington Post] Business section, Stan wrote a wonderful book called *How to Retire Happy*. He did." I think they'll be able to say that about me, too.

I retired nearly ten years ago as an investor relations executive at a local New York Stock Exchange medical device company following more than 25 years as a marketing communications practitioner in an Orange County pharmaceutical company.

"Stan wrote a wonderful book called *How to Retire Happy*. He did. I think they'll be able to say that about me, too."

Since then, I have employed my marketing communication experience in the not-for-profit sector donating my time and travel trying to pay back the blessings and grace that I received during a 40-plus-year career in the private sector.

My work has been with two separate but related institutions—first, with my local parish of the Episcopal Church and second with the Anglican Communion, the London-based international parent organization of the Episcopal Church in the United States.

Here in Orange County, I have served four three-year terms on the church's governing body, one as its leader, one as its second in command, and two as its communications director. While the resources available and decision-making process are much different from those of the private sector, we have somehow managed to enter the 21st century with our communication efforts—but only recently. While I am on the governing board—we call it the Vestry in the Episcopal Church—I tend to spend two to three hours a day with my assigned tasks. I mostly work from home remotely connected to a computer in the parish which lets me complete my work—except for meetings, of course—by walking into my home office.

This remote connection also allows me to work at the local parish from Seattle, where my children and three grandchildren live. I'm spending three or four months of the year living in a condominium that's reasonably close to both families.

About two years after I joined the local parish in 1998, our minister introduced me to a friend of his who was developing a support group for the archbishop of Canterbury called the Compass Rose Society. (The mariner's compass rose is the logo of the Communion signifying its reach throughout the world. The Anglican Communion is the fourth largest Christian communion with 85 million members, founded in 1867 in London, England.) Shortly after this meeting, I joined the Society, and our parish followed. I attended my first Annual Meeting in London in 2002 and have attended it ever since.

At first, I just watched and listened, trying to understand the Society's work, but eventually, the Board asked if I could help with their communications, and I continue to do this today. We publish a newsletter once or twice a year, depending on the budget., and with a membership of about 400 Anglicans located primarily in the US, Canada, and Hong Kong, we are heavily involved in social media, which facilitates our communication. And, of course, there are solicitations for contributions and new members, church conventions, an annual report, and other occasional member outreach notices. I probably spend at least eight hours a week on average doing this type of work.

Key Takeaways from Volunteers/Philanthropists

These philanthropists are the real thing, each committed to supporting favorite causes with time, talent, and treasure. I'm impressed that none of them waited until achieving some milestone in life to begin. For many in the middle of a career with other family obligations, their giving is modest relative to wealthier peers. But their gifts are still significant to them, and as they see the impact, they often "stretch" their giving into larger and larger amounts. The reward they each receive depends not on the size of the gift but on the significance each placed on it. Some have used their good fortune to benefit those in need while others have created greater success in order to be more generous. But all of them are fulfilled philanthropists helping to make our world a better place. (Did you spot Social Entrepreneurs in the stories of Charles Antis, Doug Edwards, and LeLani Quiray?)

CHAPTER THREE

NON-PROFIT FOUNDERS/LEADERS

For some, addressing pressing community needs is an all-consuming passion (they must have that passion to take on all they do). Starting or running a non-profit organization takes on the unyielding belief that the cause is important, the specific organization's mission unique, and the impact sought (and hopefully realized) is critical. Much of the work is like that of other entrepreneurs or business CEOs, with one significant distinction: most non-profits (many "social enterprises" excepted) will not generate more earned revenue (sales of products or services) than expenses, thus creating the ongoing need to raise funds. So in addition to adroitly addressing the community's needs, these non-profit leaders must also be able to continually attract the resources necessary to complete their mission. And they won't be able to attract those resources (unlike their for-profit peers) by promising to share the great riches earned through their business success. To survive and continue their work, they must appeal to the shared belief that the cause is important, the organization's mission unique, and that they make a significant impact. If they do that well, they create a legacy that will long be remembered in their communities, and they certainly will have lived a much richer life.

Jerri Rosen

In 1990, I was President of J.L. Rosen & Company, blending 25+ years of marketing communications experience in developing results-oriented planned giving and development programs for non-profit organizations. At the same time, I started my ad agency, five friends and I found ourselves disturbed by the growing statistics of domestic violence. The group set out on a mission to help.

Intending to host a one-time-only event, we held the first-ever "Day of Self-Esteem™," which served 67 women from six shelters. The event became the launching pad for Working Wardrobes. In 1995, the organization received official non-profit status, and in 2000 I was hired on as the Executive Director and Founder.

> **"Not one to retire, I have created a 'rewired' life that is full and fun."**

I became CEO and let my organization through some challenges, focusing always on helping thousands of men, women, veterans, and young adults each year re-enter the workforce with career development services and professional wardrobing. In 2012, the work expanded with the addition of the Veterans Network (VetNet), a safety net for veterans, who are offered full wraparound services to transition into the civilian workforce.

In a nod to my entrepreneurial spirit, Working Wardrobes operates many successful social enterprises including two upscale resale boutiques and two outlet shops, which account for more than 35% of the organization's budget. The shops have a very small paid staff and a team of volunteers who support the sales and customer service values that are so important to retail success.

For my ongoing dedication to the community, I have been recognized by civic leaders, government officials, and organizations at the national, state, and community levels. As the host of an award-winning cable TV show about Working Wardrobes, I leveraged my expertise in advertising, sales, marketing, and public relations. I am an effective and entertaining presenter and speak to many corporate and community groups in my ongoing effort to build awareness of the Working Wardrobes mission in our community.

I was more than ready to celebrate the 30th anniversary of Working Wardrobes in 2020 when the organization experienced a devasting loss—a four-alarm fire destroyed everything they owned in a leased 26,000 building. This time it was the Orange County community that provided support to Working Wardrobes and me. With outstanding financial support from the top local corporations and generous donors, along with hundreds of new donors who contributed great quality clothing, in five short months, I rebuilt my organization during the COVID crisis that affected every single person in the world.

Working Wardrobes now has a Donation Center in Irvine and a well-appointed Career Success Center in Santa Ana. Tours are regularly scheduled, and I would welcome everyone to come for a tour!

Now, in its 32 years, Working Wardrobes has served over 115,000 clients in Orange, Los Angeles, Riverside, and San Diego counties in partnership with 50 local shelters and social service agencies. With my rebuilt organization on firm ground, I chose to retire on December 31, 2021. Not one to retire, I have created a "rewired" life that is full and fun.

I took on the Chair of Executive Coaches of Orange County and am bringing my leadership and organizational skills to create a firmer foundation for the 18-year-old group. New coaches and new processes are exciting additions as the organization continues to serve non-profit executives and emerging leaders, a very important asset in our community.

I also serve as vice-chair in my new community, Reata Glen, and have developed a wider set of friends. My Board work continues with service to WISE (Women Investing in Security and Education) and The Invisible Theatre in Tucson, AZ. My current passport is always ready for another trip as I thoroughly enjoyed seeing the radiant tulips in Amsterdam and the sights in Berlin this April.

A very full life of service, remarkable friendships, love, and joy.

Antoinette Balta

I come from a large and hardworking family. My mother, born to a tribe of farmers, is the first of nine children and her father, born in the inner city, is the youngest of six. Seeking a life of stability, her parents immigrated to the United States where I was born, and afforded all the opportunities of the American Dream.

Encouraged by my mother, I am among the first women in my family to get an education holding a degree in Business Administration with an emphasis in Marketing and Management from Chapman University School of Business as well as a Juris Doctor with a special certificate in Alternative Dispute Resolution, and an LLM emphasized in Business and Economics from Chapman University Fowler School of Law.

> **". . . an exciting aspect of my job is rallying volunteers for the cause. In my own words, 'it takes a village,' and I am constantly looking to rally more troops!"**

I was raised in the Catholic Church to which I credit, along with my parents, my desire to serve. As a strong patriot grateful for all the opportunities afforded me by the United States, I have a special place in my heart for the U.S. military. I am a reserve JAG Officer with the California State Guard, previously assigned to Legal Support Command where I held the rank of Major for five years before being transferred to Strategic Communications to assist with the rebranding of the California Military Department.

Noticing an influx of service members returning from Iraq and Afghanistan seeking shelter at a local National Guard armory, I discovered that many issues that contributed to these veterans' chronic homelessness were legal and required the assistance of an attorney. Wanting to help and so moved by the fact that the men and women who had served the country abroad were now struggling, I committed myself to the cause of removing "chronic" from "homelessness" and empowering veterans into self-sufficiency. This led me to be instrumental in the co-development of a veteran-based project at a local legal aid, with over 700 veterans receiving legal assistance during my three-year tenure. Realizing the need for a military-specific legal aid that solely focuses on the military, I co-founded the Veterans Legal Institute (VLI) in 2014 where I am presently the Executive Director. Veterans Legal Institute is a non-profit law firm that provides free legal services to low-income and homeless veterans and empowers them into self-sufficiency. To date, VLI has served over 6,000 local, low-income veterans.

I am a graduate of the 2018 Presidential Leadership Scholars Class, a prestigious program that catalyzes a diverse network of leaders brought together to collaborate and make a difference in the world as they learn about leadership through the lens of the presidential experiences of George W. Bush, Bill Clinton, George H.W. Bush, and Lyndon B. Johnson. In line with my commitment to service, during my tenure in this program, I focused on the improvement and further development of mobile legal clinics for low-income veterans, a project that is shared freely throughout the nation to promote additional services for veterans in need.

I am a two-term Director-at-Large with the Orange County Bar Association, a member of the Outreach and Pro Bono Committees, and a member of the Orange County Women's Lawyers Association. I am also a Board Advisor for the National Association of Veteran-Serving Organizations and Integrated Recovery Foundation, a group dedicated to providing housing and mental health service to women survivors of military sexual assault. I am a member of the OC Veterans and Military Families Collaborative, Chair of its Legal/ Re-Entry Working Group, and for a long period served as vice-chair of its Steering Committee. I am accredited by the Department of Veterans Affairs and regularly lecture on legal topics affecting veterans, where I am known for providing innovative solutions aimed at veteran empowerment and self-sufficiency. In the past, I was a law lecturer at UCI School of Law for its Veterans Law Clinic.

I remain committed to serving heroes in need through the VLI. Apart from serving veterans, an exciting aspect of my job is rallying volunteers for the cause. In my own words, "it takes a village," and I am constantly looking to rally more troops! If you're interested in learning more about VLI, please visit **www.vetslegal.org** or email me at **abalta@vetslegal.com.**

Bill Bracken

I had no idea. No idea about the impact that my decision to create and start Bracken's Kitchen would have on so many people. I guess there are a lot of people walking through life wondering if there isn't something more. Something more meaningful, something more heartfelt, or just something more that they should be doing. "What is the meaning of life?" is a question that has been asked for generations. After all, deep inside every one of us is a longing and desire to know that in some small way, it has made a difference that we have lived.

People often ask me about my decision to walk away from a successful career as a semi-celebrity chef to feed the homeless and less fortunate. I certainly couldn't have chosen a new career path with more of a contrast from my past life. I have gone from feeding celebrities, movie stars, and presidents to feeding street people and the working poor in our communities and I have never been happier. God has truly blessed me through this.

While I know it is common and cool for sports stars to point up to God when they do something great on the field of play, but in my case, my story is pretty simple, God truly did for me what I couldn't do for myself.

You see, I was always a slave to money. Not because I needed fancy things, but because of the immense fear and insecurity in being able to provide for my family. I attribute this to the time in my childhood when my father's company, ironically Seitz Foods, was on strike and he was not working. My bedroom was closest to the kitchen, and I remember lying in bed at night while mom and dad sat at the kitchen table trying to figure out how they would get by. They worked so hard to ensure that we kids had all we needed and never went without, but those times were very tough. There were many nights when dinner was a slice of white bread and some soup poured over the top, i.e.: SOS, "Stuff on a Shingle."

"Despite the stress of it all, it was truly an immense rebirth of sorts. No longer was I a slave to corporate America—I was free."

I believe it was that time in my life that created this immense pressure to earn a decent living and provide for my family that drove me. That and the desire to make my father proud of me. I am not sure how a country boy from a town of a little over 1,000 people ended up in Beverly Hills, but I did. Along the way, I got caught up in the career rat race. After all, I lived in Southern California and worked in Beverly Hills and Newport Beach for more than 25 years.

What you wear, what you drive, where you dine, and whom you hang out with was the world I worked in. A world is driven by the success which is defined by the size of your bank account. Don't get me wrong, there is absolutely nothing wrong with success and wealth, but when the drive and desire to achieve it blinds you to what is happening around you, there is a problem.

I got caught up in that to some degree and lost my way. My focus on my success and fear of providing for my own family caused me to have a blind eye and lack of compassion for those with so much less. That drive to succeed and make dad proud fueled me and was my only priority.

When our economy took a huge hit in 2008–2010, I watched many really good people lose their jobs. While the place I was working was still making a profit and doing okay, friends were let go and struggled to get by. And I mean struggled. There were no jobs to be found. To see a grown man with a wife and two kids not be able to buy their child a Christmas present and barely put a meal on the table—that affected me. I knew then that I was being called to serve and help but didn't know how and quite frankly, was too afraid. I was tasked with unbelievable expectations, and out of fear for my financial survival, I put my head down and did what I was asked. I became detached and unfazed by the struggles of the people who worked for me. I was too worried about my future to worry about theirs.

Then the unthinkable happened. At 48 years of age, I was fired for the first time. I was walked off the property like a common criminal and thrust into the lines of the unemployed. The fear, shock, and dismay of being unemployed didn't last long as I knew it was my calling. Losing my job in December was truly one of the bigger blessings in my life. I got to enjoy Christmas off with my family for the first time in my adult life. I was invited and able to attend a New Year's Eve party. I have never been to one before then. I was always cooking. What a blessing!

While I struggled with many fears and emotions of being a 48-year-old unemployed chef, I knew it was part of a bigger story. The real fear was that my profession was a young man's game, and here I was—old and out of work. Despite the stress of it all, it was truly an immense rebirth of sorts. No longer was

I a slave to corporate America—I was free. I highly recommend it to anyone caught in the corporate whirlpool!

Soon after my departure, I received many calls from people wanting to put me to work. Moving was out of the question, so I settled on a local project. While I truly wanted to focus on feeding the less fortunate, I again got caught up in the money hustle again with an investor who wanted to open a dozen restaurants. Needless to say, that project was a complete failure, and there was no doubt then that I needed to figure this feeding the less fortunate thing out.

I worked on a concept and built a business plan around a restaurant that would give back. I worked on several consulting projects to pay the bills. My wife was a trooper through it all and worked hard to help keep our family above water financially. When I lost my job, she was a stay-at-home mom raising our two-year-old. God truly blessed me with her and her willingness to do whatever she had to help me make this happen.

Looking back now, all of my early efforts and ideas had a common thread. I was desperately trying to hold onto that former life in luxury hospitality. Little did I know then that deep inside it was my ego that was fueling this need. As I tried many different things, even starting a Filipino Pastry concept, the only thing that gained traction was Bracken's Kitchen. Now I must ask you—what does a redneck country boy from Kansas know about Filipino Pastries?—but still, I tried.

When we finally landed on the concept that came to be known as Bracken's Kitchen, I started the tedious work of getting our 501(c)(3) status and building out the plan. We found out in the fall of 2013 that our application was approved and suddenly we were a bona fide non-profit. I was knee-deep in a couple of consulting projects, so Bracken's Kitchen got moved to the back burner until early 2014.

It was in the fall of 2014 when I came to the hard realization that if I was ever going to make this thing work, then I needed to focus on it full time. I think that was one of the hardest leaps of faith. To walk away from all sources of income to focus on this and not take a salary was scary but needed.

It was as if God was saying, "About time!" It was only then that things started to fall into place. Betsy ended up on our doorstep in December of 2014 as a gift from Bruce Hecker of Bruce's Catering, and that one simple act forever changed our course. No longer was 2015 going to be a year to fundraise and buy a truck. Suddenly we had one, and off we went. Our first feeding event was at Voice of the Refugee, even before we had Betsy, and once we got her, we started feeding people and never looked back.

Bracken's Kitchen looks vastly different today, and we are excited about our future, but it all truly started when I made the big, hard, and scary decision to just do it.

Ali Woodard

It's a little-known secret that there exists a pernicious cycle of teen mothers whose children often also become pregnant as teenagers. But that fact wasn't known to me, an adopted child whose birth mother was a teenager. I grew up as many southern California kids did, which made it even more difficult when I became pregnant at age 16. Embarrassed and ashamed, I told no one about my plight and "handled it" the only way I could

> **"My reward is experiencing daily the joy that comes from being able to provide this help and knowing that these teen-parent families are growing up better than they would have without the support of Fristers."**

imagine with the help of Planned Parenthood. With that behind me, I continued my life, getting a degree from Cal State Long Beach and embarking on a successful career as the executive assistant to top business executives running some of California's most successful companies.

My experience with teen pregnancy might not have greatly affected my life if I hadn't been involved at Mariners Church in Irvine. There may mentor high school girls which inevitably leads to the topic of pregnancy, bringing back the experience I had gone through. These young girls expressed their view that there was no choice in teen pregnancy other than abortion. I knew they needed support, information, and choices and I wondered what I could do.

Then came the service at Mariners Church on ways to volunteer in our community. I listened to the service and the call to get involved, including the request to mentor pregnant and parenting teens. When I came forward, I was told no program like that existed at the church, but I also was asked if I would start one. Hesitant but excited about the opportunity, I first established partnerships with pregnancy centers and shelters for pregnant women and mobilized volunteers to provide ancillary services such as baby showers and craft nights. Seeing no other support in the community for these teens, I began the Club Mom program to provide parenting and life skills classes. This program ultimately was the beginning of Fristers, a non-profit dedicated to breaking the cycle of poverty and abuse within the teen parent population by providing education, access to resources, role models, and support.

Today, some 15 years from that Club Mom experience, Fristers has helped over 900 teen mothers and 1,000 children. Moms are graduating high school, enrolling in college and vocational training programs, getting their driver's licenses, securing employment, and becoming responsible, caring parents to their children. And children are receiving early intervention services that are improving their developmental, social, and educational gains. Recently Fristers expanded programming to include teen fathers and teen parent couples, strengthening the entire family. Now alumni of the program (graduates who complete three or more years in the program and must graduate high school) are helping as volunteers and donors. And Fristers is looking to launch its programs and services into new communities throughout Orange County.

As for me, I believe that running Fristers is what I was born to do, my calling. I took my experience and a desire to help others and created an organization helping hundreds get the help and support unavailable to me as a teen. My reward is experiencing daily the joy that comes from being able to provide this help and knowing that these teen-parent families are growing up better than they would have without the support of Fristers.

Dawn S. Reese, CFRE

My journey to **The Wooden Floor** is "doing the work I love; with people I love.

After graduating with a bachelor's degree in Psychology from California State University Long Beach, I had planned to return to college to become a teacher and eventually a school principal. As life would take a turn shortly after graduation, I began working for my sorority sister's father Randal Walti to build a CEO coaching and management consulting firm for the technology sector. Over the next 10 years, I remained at the firm and built my business skills in finance, human resources, business development, and marketing, so I didn't return to get my teaching credential. However, what I learned in those years through Randal and other mentors has been instrumental to where I am today as a "mission-driven, business-minded" non-profit leader.

"I believe our students will become change agents and beacons of hope within their own families, their neighborhoods, our community, and our world. "

Randal focused on blending Christian and business principles that still influence my work every day. He believed in giving back to the community as one of our corporate values. Only in my 20s, did I volunteer with the **Torrance Chamber of Commerce** in their elementary school character-building program, and I was on the Board of Directors for the **Torrance Symphony** and the **South Bay Children's Health Center.** Randal and I founded a non-profit trade association called the **Software Council of Southern California,** and I served as the first Executive Director.

Little did I know those experiences years ago in the arts, education, children's services, and governance would blend and lead me directly to the work I do at The Wooden Floor.

The Wooden Floor is taking an innovative approach to youth development as we transform the lives of youth in underserved communities through the power of dance and access to higher education. In Orange County and through our nationally licensed partners, we use a long-term approach grounded in exploratory dance education strategically integrated with academics, college, and career readiness, as well as family services. Our goal is to foster the resources within each child to innovate, communicate, and collaborate – skills necessary for success in school and life. **Since 2005, 100 percent of students who graduate from The Wooden Floor immediately enroll in higher education.** I believe our students will become change agents and beacons of hope within their own families, their neighborhoods, our community, and our world.

For our students, The Wooden Floor becomes a second home for up to 10 years. We get the privilege to help each student, and their parents navigate the transitions between elementary, middle, high school, and college. Because of the long-term relationship we have with each family, they become like family members to us. We care deeply about them and their challenges due to their socio-economic hardships. We are here for them when they need us.

At The Wooden Floor, I love the work I do with the people I get to work with and in-service for. What is more important than moving young people forward both in school and in life? There is no better time for me than 4:00 pm when the gates of our campus swing open when the children arrive. From where my office sits, I have a direct vantage point to see the coming and goings of our students. Backpacks swing off, and students begin to do their homework at the tables in the courtyard before dance classes or their tutoring sessions. Parents arrive to bring snacks for their children or to volunteer. One of my favorite parts of my day is to go out to greet them and say hello or peek inside the studio when they are taking classes. I like to ask them how they are doing with their schoolwork, friends, and in general to encourage them.

I am honored to work with a generous and loving community of Board members, staff, and supporters of individuals, corporations, as well as private and family foundations. We are united as one to ensure our students know: that from here you can step anywhere.

Upon recent reflection, I realized that through my work at The Wooden Floor I am similar in many ways to a teacher and a principal for the young people and their families that we serve every day! Lifting children out of poverty to achieve their full potential has become my life's purpose.

Jennifer Friend

A 12-year-old girl sitting on a motel bed, surrounded by homework, siblings, and parents, all crammed into one small room. A 9-year-old boy enters a classroom with his head down, ashamed to not know where he will sleep tonight.

These are the images of children in Orange County struggling with homelessness—the county's best-kept secret. While we may not see these motel kids along the streets or desperately gripping cardboard signs, they exist in overwhelming abundance.

Under the area's veil of affluence are the faces of more than 32,500 children experiencing homelessness and 120,000 children living in poverty. They say goodnight from motels, shelters, and couches. They are forced to focus on where they will sleep instead of what they will learn. Tragically, their educations and futures suffer.

> **"Feelings of shame, lack of privacy, and an economically schizophrenic childhood created an environment where the basic elements of being a kid were sometimes lost, like doing homework."**

Years ago, I was one of these faces. For decades I silenced my past as an Orange County motel kid, but in the spring of 2013, I shared my story to spark hope and conversation about dealing with childhood homelessness.

A technology entrepreneur, my father experienced unpredictable lapses in income. Although my mother also worked as a preschool teacher, keeping a roof over our family of six proved taxing. While there were periods of financial stability, there were also times of despair.

During my junior high and high school years, my three brothers, our parents, and I often packed our lives into 214-square-foot motel rooms. Feelings of shame, lack of privacy, and an economically schizophrenic childhood created an environment where the basic elements of being a kid were sometimes lost, like doing homework.

Childhood homelessness data from the U.S. Department of Education is shocking. According to the department, 1 in 30 children in the country experienced homelessness in 2013.

On a local level, here in Orange County, it's 1 in 6. California has the largest population of homeless children in America, and Orange County has more homeless students than the state average than neighboring Los Angeles and San Diego counties, per the California Department of Education.

The effects of youth homelessness are devastating, ranging from chronic emotional stress and physical malnourishment to significant academic gaps and difficulty making friends. In comparison with their peers, children experiencing homelessness are nine times more likely to repeat a grade, four times more likely to drop out of school, and three times more likely to be placed in special education programs, according to The Institute for Children, Poverty, and Homelessness.

But there is hope.

At Project Hope Alliance we start with the kids. Our goal is to ensure that every homeless child in Orange County succeeds academically.

Our impactful, two-generational approach ends homelessness today by rapidly rehousing the families we serve and helping them achieve financial independence. We end the cycle of generational homelessness tomorrow by empowering our kids with a unique academic program lovingly tailored to their skills and strengths.

Three especially notable programs are our innovative Bright Start Pilot Program, the Promoter Pathway program at Newport Harbor High School, and our core Family Stability Program.

Since 2012, we have ended homelessness for more than 700 kids and parents by stabilizing families in their own homes and providing their children with an exceptional education.

Take my story as an example of the boundless power of faith, hope, and determination. Since graduating from UC Irvine and Whittier Law School, becoming a partner at a large law firm before age 40, then leaving the practice of law to proudly serve as Project Hope Alliance's CEO, I have realized that my story is not about me. I just happen to be the one with a voice right now to communicate that a child's future should never be determined by their parents' economic circumstances.

I look ahead to our third annual gala on April 17 with hope and purpose. Project Hope Alliance exists to mend the chaos in the lives of children and families struggling with homelessness and to ensure that they never, ever give up.

Learn more about how we endure ending the cycle of homelessness, one child at a time, at **projecthopealliance.org.**

Jennifer Friend is CEO of the Project Hope Alliance.

Je'net Kreitner

I have a great story of turning life's harshest lessons into life's greatest blessings. Shortly after a very poor relationship ended badly, my young son and I were dropped on the side of the road with nowhere to go. My son and I became part of the growing homeless population. After a hopeless six months of struggling to survive on the streets and bouncing from one motel to another, an angel entered my life.

A man I had met briefly saw something in me as he visited with me, goodness and potential that many overlooked because of my circumstances. After visiting with me only once, he offered to take me and my son into his home. His faith in me and the help he offered us allowed me to land back on my feet, and eventually, he became my husband.

> **"Shortly after a very poor relationship ended badly, my young son and I were dropped on the side of the road with nowhere to go."**

I began my incredible journey to pay it forward at a monthly Homeless Outreach program offered at my church in Orange, California, as well as participating in the Gleaners Jail Ministry Program. But after the death of my mother, I wanted to do more and began by taking a woman into my home whom I had befriended at a bus stop. The woman lived with me and my family for a few months until they could find an apartment and help her get back on her feet.

After that, the guest room in our home was constantly occupied with people whom I wanted to help. One day my husband remarked that there were more of these "guests" living in our house than family members. So, I did the only thing that seemed to make sense, I, my husband, and my children moved out of the house and turned it into the very first shelter in 2004.

It was then that Grandma's House of Hope was founded as an effort to give back to a community that aided me in rebuilding my life after I was homeless in 1991. The purpose of Grandma's House of Hope is to "Empower the Invisible," helping women (and recently men, with the opening of Grandpa's House) to recover, heal and move forward in their lives. In addition to Grandma's House, I also founded a healing house program for homeless women with cancer.

Providing a home to these women allows them to enter chemotherapy programs that are unavailable to those that cannot provide a house address or other proof that they are not homeless. Other programs under Grandma's House of Hope include a pregnancy shelter, housing for women with mental illnesses whose medications cause them to fail drug tests, and people with disabilities who are unable to work. In 2007, Grandma's House of Hope officially became a non-profit organization.

I did not stop by just helping adults. Inspired by the haunting memory of my own child's hunger when we were homeless, I founded the Nana's Kidz Program. This program provides meals to children who live in motels over the weekend and during the summer when they cannot receive a meal from school programs.

I also started the Hope Works Education and Enrichment Center, which is an after-school program for high-risk kids in low-income neighborhoods. This program keeps children off the streets and out of gangs in an area with high rates of gang activity. Through my various programs, we have rescued and restored over 2,000 women, served over two million meals, and reached over 20,000 families.

Lisa Ackerman

In September 1999, the word "autism" rang through my ears like a cannon shot across the bow. My husband and I knew something was not going well with our son Jeff, but we would have never guessed it was autism.

Following that fateful visit with the neurologist, we visited many other professionals, including medical doctors, speech pathologists, audiologists, and behaviorists. The list seemed endless. The common message we were given is Autism has no hope, no cure. The first three medical doctors recommended that my family find "institutional placement" for Jeff who was at the ripe old age of two and a half years years at the time.

> **"In September 1999, the word 'autism' rang through my ears like a cannon shot across the bow. "**

Refusing to give up on our son, my husband and I spent hundreds of hours talking to any parents of a child diagnosed with autism, reading dozens of recommended books, watching countless hours of educational videos, and constantly surfing the Internet. Of course, surfing the Internet constantly. We were determined that our beloved son would grow far beyond his label and that he would have a future that was wonderful and amazing despite his autism diagnosis. Early on, the most important step for us was to GET BUSY. It was up to us, HIS PARENTS, to make a difference in his future.

The early days of our son's diagnosis were frustrating. Those countless hours spent researching, reading, talking—wasn't there a better way? Wasn't there SOMEONE who had already done the same research and search for answers before, who could have brought us up to speed much sooner for us to help our son faster?

Fast forward to November 2000, when our daughter Lauren (at the advanced age of 16) recommended that we start a parent support group. Both my husband and I felt we were not qualified. Still, we wanted the company of other families going through the same struggles so we could both socialize and share information, especially new research and treatment options as they become available.

We also hoped to build a community where parents would be:

- Inspired by each other's steadfast hopes for their children's futures

- Passionate about autism education for themselves and other similarly struggling families

- Enthusiastic about raising awareness about autism in the general public

The Autism Community in Action (TACA) began with 10 families in a living room in 2000. In 2022, we will serve well over 83,000 families around the United States. From grassroots beginnings in Southern California, TACA expanded nationwide and now has a physical presence via our Chapters and provides a virtual offering for all families facing an autism diagnosis.

Where is my son Jeff now? He is in his last year of college at his first-choice university. He talks, makes jokes, plays multiple instruments, composes his songs, socializes with typical friends, and is an active member of society with a bright future. He is the sweetest, kindest person I know and is practically always smiling. That is a far cry from his early diagnosis and the initial prognosis for his future.

TACA's goal is to provide education, support, and information to parents to help their children diagnosed with autism be the very best they can be, with the hope of recovery and or independence.

Today, there are many, many medical treatments and therapeutic options that help alleviate many of the symptoms suffered by our children diagnosed with autism. Let us share our collective, hard-won knowledge and experience with your family so your child's treatment can begin right away. Ask about the autism journey because we are families with autism who have already "been there and done that" with many of our children. Some of us still work hard every day with our children for whom we never give up hope.

We are **Families with Autism Helping Families with Autism.** The autism journey is not an easy one. It's a marathon, not a sprint, so take each minute, hour, or day, one at a time. It will be difficult, but it will also be incredibly rewarding because it will change your life, your family's life, and most importantly, the lives of your children with autism to all enjoy a brighter future.

I wish all families treating and caring for their children with autism the very best possible outcomes for their children as they continue forward on the journey.

Michelle Wulfesteig

I had my first stroke when I was eleven years old, which led to the diagnosis of a rare vascular brain lesion, known as an Arteriovenous Malformation (AVM), or a tangle of blood vessels and arteries. With no other options, I underwent two very intense forms of radiation, which caused permanent paralysis to the right side of my body. I had to learn how to do everything with my left hand as I mourned the loss of all the activities I used to be able to do—running, playing sports, and just being a kid.

> **"So, at the age of 14, I decided to live every day to the fullest, knowing that I had a limited life expectancy. "**

The plan was to have a third radiation treatment, but the doctors thought it would cause more damage than good. My family explored all the options, but in every scenario, the risks outweighed the benefits., and if they opted for traditional surgery, the doctors said I probably wouldn't survive the operation. So, at the age of 14, I decided to live every day to the fullest, knowing that I had a limited life expectancy.

In high school, I tried out for volleyball and made the team. Skipping my way around the court to get the ball, Michelle even learned to serve with one hand. During college, I traveled the world where I, climbed the Great Wall of China, saw the Taj Mahal, and went on safari in Africa.

It seemed I had outwitted my short life sentence. Then, on January 4, 2008, I suffered a second devastating stroke. This time it nearly took my life as I slipped into a deep coma. The doctors didn't have much hope. They had no choice but to surgically remove the lesion lodged deep inside my brain. My family was told that I might never wake up, and if I did, I would not be able to walk, talk or see.

For eight days, my family waited. To the world, I was unresponsive, trapped by an unyielding coma. But what they didn't see is that my spirit had been transported to a place of prayers, surrounded by God's light. The experience brought me an overwhelming sense of peace, giving me the comfort I had never known.

And then the miracle of healing that I had been praying for all my life happened. I awoke—free from the lesion that had threatened to end my life. Through this experience, I learned that living and dying are closely intertwined and that sometimes, we must face our mortality before we can appreciate just how precious each moment is because, in the end, all we have is today.

Now recovered, but still physically disabled, I am the Executive Director of the Southern California Hospice Foundation (SCHF) a non-profit organization dedicated to enhancing the lives of terminally ill patients and their families. For those struggling financially, food is provided, and overdue bills are paid. Homeless patients are clothed and treated with dignity. Veterans are honored and given a final salute. Families are reunited to say their goodbyes. Children and adults alike are granted their last wish. And grieving families gain support from our frequent bereavement workshops.

I recently launched a capital campaign to create a loving home for the last stage, a place that will be funded entirely by philanthropic dollars. A place where not a single person will be turned away due to lack of funds. A place where dignity and compassion reign.

Today, I hope to be an inspiration to those who are struggling. My greatest wish is that you'll find your true purpose, using the gifts you were given to change a life, make a difference, do good, and be all you can be.

You can learn more about my remarkable story in my award-winning memoir, "All We Have Is Today," or become involved with the Southern California Hospice Foundation by visiting **www.socalhospicefoundation.org.**

Penny Lambright

I am the founder of the non-profit organization "Patriots and Paws" in Anaheim, California. Lambright collects used household items and gives them to vets. I invite them to "shop" at a warehouse, but no money is required because everything is free. My vision and philanthropic way of thinking have genuinely changed the lives of thousands of veterans in Orange County.

I am no stranger to military life and the effects of war. I was the daughter of a U.S. Marine whose father had fought in WWII and the Korean War. As the youngest of five siblings, I was often known as a take-action kind of girl, a trait that has certainly followed me throughout my life.

Helping Others

I started "Patriots and Paws" in 2011 after receiving a $125,000 inheritance. At the time, my nephew had just returned home from his second tour of duty in the Middle East. When he came home, he told me how his fellow soldiers were coming home with nothing and needed help.

At the time, I was running my professional company but began to collect items for Veterans in my spare time. I used my inheritance to rent a storage unit, which quickly filled up. I rented another, which quickly turned into six due to the overwhelming support and response. That's when I moved the organization to a warehouse in Orange to store all the donations and provide a larger area for the veterans to shop. They have since moved into a much larger location in Anaheim.

Despite the COVID-19 pandemic, my organization has still flourished as it continues to collect donations and help vets in need. I have helped more than 9,000 vets get the necessary supplies they need for their homes.

Bringing Pets and Vets Together

Besides having a love for helping others, I also have a love for animals. This Is why I currently work to pair rescue dogs with vets through community partners. Future plans include having a kennel where Veterans can kennel their animals at no cost, so they take care of their own needs like housing or medical/ legal needs. That's where the paws part of the organization comes in.

"I invite them to "shop" at a warehouse, but no money is required because everything is free."

I believe animals can help humans in complex situations just as much as humans can help animals.

Although I am plenty busy running the organization and running my professional organizing company, I still find time to spread joy to others.

I have also created a "Leave Your Burden Behind Wall" near the warehouse. This is a fence I built out of pallets where vets are invited to write a message. They are encouraged to write about any burden that bothers them and to leave it on the wall. This is a way to let go of any problems people may face.

My investment in the community goes far beyond using every penny of my inheritance to start Patriots and Paws. My selflessness, vision, and desire to help those in need are an inspiration and model for others in Orange County and beyond.

Stephanie Courtillier

My fellow entrepreneurs, it's not about doing more. It's about being more of *yourself*. I'm Stephanie Courtillier, and I learned this the hard way. As an ambitious workaholic, I leaped into entrepreneurship headfirst.

Millions of half-baked ideas littered my brain. I chased what everybody else was doing so I, too, could achieve (seemingly) overnight success. In true ENFJ fashion, I built on too many projects simultaneously and gave up when they didn't work quickly enough.

Or I took the opposite route and analyzed/paralyzed each idea, so it never got off the ground. Either way, I had little to no results to show.

Burnout mode hit me like a ton of bricks—several times. Since our businesses are an extension of ourselves, I started questioning everything about my true worth as a person.

Why am I constantly having to prove myself? How do I stop people-pleasing and start believing in myself? Who am I, as a mom? Who am I, as a business owner? Who am I?

How do I integrate giving back, so it doesn't feel like I'm running a charity AND a business? Can I be financially stable and live my social impact dreams at the same time?

The worst part was that I appeared "successful" to everyone on the outside. Yet, I was frustrated, tired, and didn't see a clear path to live up to the potential I KNEW was inside of me. The shift happened when I sat down with myself and asked, what's MY version of a fulfilled life? I realized it wasn't about finding success. Instead, I needed to find SIGNIFICANCE.

"Why am I constantly having to prove myself? How do I stop people-pleasing and start believing in myself? Who am I, as a mom? Who am I, as a business owner? Who am I?"

It was time to stop looking outward for the answers. I just had to get quiet, borrow my community's belief in me, and go deep inside to design my pathway to fulfillment. I took action in ways that scared me, like competing (and winning!) in speech competitions, integrating trauma-informed personal development work, hiring a virtual assistant, and investing 10k in a mastermind—even though that's exactly how much I had earned that year from my business.

Each step opened new doors.

I learned my superpower: designing communities that create connection and impact so each member thrives. After honing in on my calling, I started seeing tremendous results in my business.

I want every female entrepreneur who's stuck questioning their worth to realize their full potential.

Integrous Women is the result of years of conversations, training, lived experiences, and dreams. Our Pathway to Fulfillment Membership provides a home to women traveling the journey of entrepreneurship who feel out of alignment with their deeper purpose—why they started their business in the first place.

Through our 6-step Fulfillment Formula, our Pathfinders design the impact we want to be and make through our businesses, not by doing more, but by being more of ourselves.

We are coaches who practice launching their social impact-driven offer, photographers who finally step out from behind the camera to be seen by their audience, and entrepreneurs who speak to their largest audience. Integrous Women is a playground of like-hearted visionaries taking daily action to make their dreams a reality.

Key Takeaways from Non-profit Founders/Leaders

These leaders are truly inspiring. They saw important needs and committed to addressing them to the best of their abilities. In doing so, they took giant leaps of faith and great personal risks in foregoing more lucrative alternatives to make this impact. But they also demonstrate that some of the greatest rewards are realized by devoting themselves to helping others learn, grow, and prosper. I am so impressed by what they do, how they lead, and how their belief in the goodness of so many sustains them as they shepherd an idea into an enduring, mission-driven organization that changes so many lives for the better. They, perhaps more than any others, make it possible for so many *to live richer lives.*

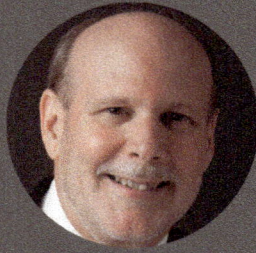

Richard J. Ward

I'm so blessed; I get to live such a full, rich life every day. Central is my practice advising individuals on envisioning and living a most rewarding future. Everyone is different, and helping them define what will bring the greatest personal rewards is such an interesting undertaking. And in learning what people are interested in doing, I can find so many places where I'm engaged that they may find rewarding. Daily, helping them live these lives and teaching them how they can be more effective philanthropists is great fun.

Beyond my professional practice, I get to be involved with so many important causes that are changing lives for the better as well.

Most recently, I served for four years as the Chairman of the Board of Governors at Center Club Orange County. In this capacity, I led a 25-person Board of Governors in its role of representing the 800+ members to the club's management. We created programming, developed and managed a charitable grant program, and helped recruit new members to the club.

For the past five years and continuing in 2022, I have been a member of the Orange County Community Foundation's Impact Philanthropy Group. Each year this group adopts a cause or theme, research organizations addressing the cause, and grants to the best candidates impacting the theme.

For several years now, I've been a chapter leader for Orange County Advisors in Philanthropy, a group of professionals who work to promote philanthropy through education, training, and relationship building. I became President of this chapter from 2022 through 2023.

Most significantly, I have been involved for several years with OneOC, a leading non-profit organization dedicated to accelerating non-profit success. I founded and led a volunteer leadership council that promotes volunteerism throughout our community. I joined the OneOC Board of Directors in 2019 and 2022. I added the role of a member of its Governance Committee, which directs and manages the organization's leadership and management, and co-chair the External Connections Committee.

I also continue to serve as a member of the Advisory Board for the Passkey Foundation's Institute for Community Impact, which focuses on those helping to improve their communities.

"This theme is consistent with the values I hold most dear, namely freedom, generosity, and service. I make every effort to focus my time, treasure, and talent on supporting these values however I can."

And beginning in 2022, I will also be hosting outreach events for Hillsdale College, which believes in and promotes the diffusion of learning essential to the perpetuity of civil and religious liberty. It focuses on preserving and teaching Western philosophy and heritage, finding its most explicit expression in the American experiment of self-government under law.

All of these organizations present great opportunities for me to impact the world by expanding the reach of philanthropy and volunteerism. This theme is consistent with the values I hold most dear, namely freedom, generosity, and service. I make every effort to focus my time, treasure, and talent on supporting these values however I can. That's how I *live a richer life.*

CONCLUSIONS

My purpose in writing this book is to demonstrate how our neighbors and colleagues live a richer life and to inspire more of you to pursue these riches as well if you're not already. But there is a deeper, more important purpose.

While America is the most generous society the world has ever known, I believe we can—and should—do better. While we have created the best clothed, fed, housed, and happiest society in history, there are still too many that have fallen behind or been left out. Even affluent communities (like Orange County, California, where I live) have too many people that are not able to fully care for themselves and their families, who don't know how to get on the great train of economic success that our private business system fuels, who have trouble getting the education so necessary for being good workers, providers, and citizens. Too many diseases and afflictions without accessible cures impact our neighbors and families. There are too many social ills that victimize too many of the vulnerable. And we trust there are wondrous discoveries that will greatly advance everyone's well-being, looking for the resources to unlock their secrets.

These challenges have always been with us and likely always will be in one form or another. I believe we all are responsible for addressing these challenges to the best of our abilities to create a better society where everyone is growing, prospering, and contributing. Our collective efforts generate progress on so many fronts, improving lives and creating a better future for everyone. Some argue that the government should do this, but I do not believe the government has the creativity, insights, discipline, or management capabilities to do this well. I believe that donor-supported non-profits working to address problems and opportunities is the better alternative to government efforts, and they deserve everyone's support. I envision a world where the "haves" is generously helping the "have-nots" so that all these problems are minimized and these opportunities are maximized. What a wonderful world that will be.

But my experiences have taught me that many successful people are not participating. I don't believe this is from selfishness or indifference. I believe it is due mainly to being unaware. They do not know all the needs and opportunities. They do not know how much impact they can have. They are unfamiliar with the wonderful personal rewards, and emotional satisfaction realized when helping others in need. They may believe the government is doing all needed to address problems. They have been so focused on personal success that they haven't yet learned about the needs and ways these problems are addressed. There aren't a lot of educational programs on philanthropy offered to most of us in our daily lives. And many believe philanthropy is the sole province of the very wealthy.

All the individuals in this book share a wonderful sense of personal fulfillment, great emotional satisfaction, and valued purpose. Their contributions to others, in so many different ways, are the keys to this fulfillment while also doing so much to improve the world. These "haves" are helping many "have-nots." They are making a great impact on the world and helping to create that society I described above. I want you and many others to see their examples, understand their means, and realize how each one benefits. Hopefully, from their examples, many more will decide this is something they, too, should explore, incorporate into their lives, and embrace as a wonderful new purpose. If so, I will have furthered my purpose and mission of helping even more live a richer life.

So, what kind of impact will you make?

How will you live a richer life?

ABOUT THE AUTHOR

Richard J. Ward

My Halftime Story

By the time 2011 rolled around, I had spent more than 30 years providing customary financial planning services to my clients: helping do college planning and retirement analysis. This process typically revolved around determining how much a client would need to accumulate to retire, usually to go off to lead the traditional notion of living out the golden years: travel, golf, and spending time with grandchildren. While all these activities are rewarding in their own way, I saw many fall into the trap of empty days with little direction or purpose for their lives. I began to question if continuing to pursue and enable this picture of the golden years was really what would be fulfilling for me. I was feeling more and more empty and bored with this routine.

Now, by this time, I had also spent some 25 years as a volunteer leader. Thus, I was proud to help bright young students get a great start in life with a terrific education like the one I received at UCLA. I experienced the wonderment of a child experiencing her first symphony concert at our new performing arts center. I saw the sense of pride on the face of a disabled adult upon receiving his paycheck from the job training he received from Goodwill Industries. I learned that some of the greatest rewards in life were earned while helping others grow, thrive, and prosper. And I saw countless non-profit organizations striving to make our community better, stronger, and safer—often without the human and financial resources that make our economy the envy of the world.

With a positive view of the philanthropic world, I joined a new organization to further charitable impact in our communities, The International Association of Advisors in Philanthropy. At one of my first speaker events, I heard some amazing stories from unique people who had decided they wanted more from life than just the financial rewards of business. They saw a calling for themselves in using their skills, experience, and resources to help change lives for the better. I listened with amazement at the adventures they orchestrated to make a significant impact on people in our community and around the world. They also shared the surprisingly great impact these adventures also had on their lives and those of their families. As I listened, my excitement grew at the idea that these people found a better way to move from success in the business world to new, significant rewards as they moved through their second halves of life, often this period coinciding with their golden years.

I also read Bob Buford's "Finishing Well,"; wherein numerous successful people described how they made significant contributions they believed were the path to finishing their life well. It became clear to me that the secret to living life well, pursuing continued growth, and leaving a lasting legacy is found by making contributions to our communities that help others prosper. Eureka! I had found the answers to the lack of fulfillment I had been experiencing in my practice.

Having a purpose is essential for all of us. A big part of the emptiness I had been experiencing was a product, I believe, of not knowing what my purpose in life was. Now I could see it clearly. My purpose is to help people live better lives, both the "haves" and the "have-nots." The non-profit organizations I had come to know (and countless others) were helping those most in need improve their lives. Supporting and enabling these organizations would definitely help a critical part of society live better lives. At the same time, my work in growing, preserving, and helping my clients use their assets has long helped them live better lives. However, my eureka moment showed me that helping my clients find new ways to live out their golden years, to redefine retirement as they use their skills, experience, and resources to help others live better lives through charitable engagement and involvement would most definitely help them live richer lives. My sense of pride and contentment grew as I finally realized not only what I'd do with my efforts in the future but why.

One of my mentors, David Elliott, listened to my story and pointed out, simply, that I had had a "Halftime" experience wherein I went from dissatisfaction with my role in life to one of being excited to re-engage with clarity of purpose. He let me know how common this experience was for successful people at some point in their life (and I recognized it from reading Bob Buford's Halftime). With Dave encouraging me, I adopted a mission of inspiring people to find their purpose and passion by serving others through charitable causes. I knew that if I could learn how they wanted to make an impact on others, I could help them pursue this new direction with guidance, resources, and my professional skills. This new mission would focus my work and efforts as I pursued my purpose in life. This clarity of purpose, mission, and work provide great peace of mind as I wake up each day with great pride and anticipation for the activities that will come.

Now I look forward to going to work, knowing where and how I'll be able to pursue my purpose. I'm surrounded by people who understand me, my mission, and my work. Their support makes it easier to stay focused and diligent as I make efforts to help my clients and others. This makes my transition into my second half fun and enjoyable every day, wherever it leads. I certainly am living a much richer life.

9 798218 072865